MW00593523

Faith, Family & Finances

Faith, Family & Finances

Volume Two

John Marshall

Faith, Family, and Finances—Volume Two
© 2009 by John Marshall

This book or parts thereof may not be reproduced in any form, stored in a retrieval system, or transmitted in any form by any means—electronic, mechanical, photocopy, recording, or otherwise—without prior written permission of the publisher, except as provided by United States of America copyright law.

Copyright © 2009 by John Marshall
All rights reserved

Unless otherwise noted, all Scripture quotations are from the New American Standard Bible. Copyright © 1960, 1962, 1963, 1968, 1971, 1972, 1973, 1975, 1977 by the Lockman Foundation. Used by permission. (www.Lockman.org)

Cover Design and Layout: Cathleen Kwas

ISBN: 978-0-9820475-1-4
Printed in the United States of America

"Come, let us rebuild the wall of Jerusalem so that we will no longer be a reproach" (Nehemiah 2:17).

DEDICATION

I DEDICATE THIS BOOK TO DR. RUSSELL A. POINTER AND his vivacious wife, Evangeline (Gina), along with the Hickory Heights Church of Christ in Antioch, Tennessee. Russell is a native of Bronx, New York. He has been preaching the word of God since age eleven, having been brought up under the tutelage of Dr. R. C. Wells in the Harlem Church of Christ.

With a vision to evangelize, enlighten, embrace, encourage, equip, empower, and exalt the people of God, Russell stepped out in faith and planted the Hickory Heights Church of Christ, affectionately known as just "the Heights." He started out with eight members and now fellowships with a membership of more than 150. Because Russell and Gina have a heart for God and the people of God, He will certainly rain down His favor upon them and all who are at the Heights.

When Gina heard that I needed some "away time" to finish this manuscript, she quickly offered a trade: If I conducted two evenings of teacher training at the Heights, she and Russell would give me two incognito days in Nashville—room and board included. I readily accepted. Thanks to the Heights, I was able to get away and finish this project in a timely manner. Thanks to Gina, I have been able to get many of my books into the hands, heads, and hearts of the reading audience.

Although the adversities that Russell and Gina face have been numerous, God still honors the good heart of His servants. Russell, keep the faith, stay strong, and God will lead you to even greater heights. May your love abound still more and more in real knowledge and all discernment, so that you may approve the things that are excellent, in order to be sincere and blameless until the day of Christ.

TABLE OF CONTENTS

ACKNOWLEDGEMENTS

THANKS BE TO JEHOVAH GOD WHO HAS BLESSED me with every spiritual blessing in the heavenly places in Christ, predestined and adopted me as a son, and filled me with the knowledge of His will in all spiritual wisdom and understanding. To Him, be praise and honor.

Denise Baker, Andrea Griggs, and Adrianne Pless provided treasured editorial insights. Without their assistance, I would be unwilling to write.

To the thousands who have sat in audiences, know that you helped me to formulate the ideas and ideology of this book. Dialogue between us has shaped and sharpened this book's focus. I am particularly grateful to those who shared with me their personal experiences. Feeling the hurt of those who have been trampled by the very ones whom God sent to console them continually agonizes my spirit. It is that feeling that was like a "fire shut up in my bones" that would not allow me to hold my peace and compelled me to pen these words.

And, more than anyone else, my wife, Priscilla, my children, Terrence (Kristol), Marrkus (Erica), Jondreia, and Johnathan, even without their knowing it, created the climate and cultivated the soil in which my ideas germinate and grow. I love you all!

PREFACE

N 605 BC, DURING THE REIGN OF JEHOIAKIM, KING OF Judah, the Babylonian king, Nebuchadnezzar, attacked Jerusalem and deported many Jews to Babylon (see 2 Chronicles 36:5-9, 2 Kings 24:1-5). God's dedicated servant, Daniel, was numbered among those in this deportation. During the year 597 BC, during the reign of Jehoiachin, king of Judah, the Babylonian king, Nebuchadnezzar, deported more Jews to Babylon (see 2 Chronicles 36:10, 2 Kings 24:6-16). God's dedicated servant, Ezekiel, was numbered among those of this later deportation. Yet again, during the year 586 BC, during the reign of Zedekiah, king of Judah, the Babylonian king, Nebuchadnezzar, again attacked Jerusalem totally destroying the temple and the walls of Jerusalem (see 2 Chronicles 36:11-21, 2 Kings 24:17-25:30).

Thereafter, a restoration began. In 538 BC, some of the Jews returned with Zerubbabel and rebuilt the temple in Jerusalem (see Ezra 3:8). In 458 BC, eighty years later, more Jews returned to Jerusalem with the prophet Ezra (see Ezra chapters 7-8). Approximately, thirteen years later, Nehemiah returned and rebuilt the walls around Jerusalem (see Nehemiah chapters 1-3).

Long before Nehemiah returned, he heard about the desolate condition of Jerusalem (see Nehemiah 1:1-3). He talked to God about that condition (see verses 4-11) and God gave Nehemiah His vision to rebuild the walls around the city (see Nehemiah 2:11-12).

We need a Nehemiah in our day. Yes, our generation longs for someone like Nehemiah who can see the mess that we are in. "Then I said to them, 'You see the bad situation we are in, that Jerusalem is desolate and its gates burned by fire'" (Nehemiah 2:17a). Not only do we need a Nehemiah who can see the mess we are in, but we need a Nehemiah who will speak the message that will lead us out of the mess we are in. "Come, let us rebuild the wall of Jerusalem so that we will no longer be a reproach" (verse 17b). In this book we will look at three critical areas where the protective walls around us have been breached: faith, family, and finances. I promise to speak the truth to you and share what I believe is God's plan to rebuild the wall "so that we will no longer be a reproach" (verse 17).

The apocryphal book of 1 Esdras tells the story of three men selected by the king to compete in a national riddle contest. The riddle to be solved was, "What is the strongest thing in the world?" On the day of the contest, the three contestants strode out onto center stage. The first boldly declared that strong wine was the strongest thing known to man, for it had the power to control and confuse the strongest man. The second contestant declared that the king was far stronger, for he alone wields power among the nations, and kingdoms bow to his authority. The third contestant addressed the applauding audience and said, "There is one thing that is stronger than the influence of wine and more powerful than the king. It is truth. Truth is stronger than anything. Truth endures and lasts forever, long after the wine dissipates, and long after a king's rule ends. Truth lives on and prevails forever and ever."

In this book I seek to speak the truth. If this seems to be an indictment, I apologize not, for I intend it to indict. First, however, I must admit that I am not fully exculpated. Yes, as a preacher of the gospel, not only should I have said more than I have said, but I should have said more sooner than I said it.

For quite some time, I have observed how believers are boldly marching away from our purpose of helping sinners and saints to overcome sin. This book is really about where I think we are as a fellowship and as the body of Christ— and where God wants to lead our fellowship and the body of Christ. Naturally, this then includes me along with others. Therefore, I know that just as God has blessed me, He has also blessed you and many others. His blessings abundantly and continually flow down upon our fellowship. Many gracious experiences indicate God's continued guidance toward those of us who have named the name of Jesus. Do allow me, however, to speak passionately about how I think the church responds to sin and to saints who sin. Also, let me passionately speak about how we have failed to talk candidly about family and financial issues as well. Finish drinking your lemonade, tie tightly your Timberlands, and let us walk the path as I point to the pieces of the pathological paradigm that interferes with holistic healing. Therefore, in the words of the apostle Paul, in advance I ask, "So have I become your enemy by telling you the truth?" (Galatians 4:16). *Can we all get along...with truth?*

PART 1

FAITH

A S YOU READ THIS SECTION, YOU ARE LIKELY TO wonder, "What does this have to do with faith?" Through the pen of the apostle Paul, the Holy Spirit posed the question: "How then will they call on Him in whom they have not believed? How will they believe in Him whom they have not heard? And how will they hear without a preacher?" (Romans 10:14).

Did you notice how God links the preacher and his preaching in the chain of faith? Whomever or whatever dictates the preaching that you hear determines the faith you will develop. There exists not only a correlation between preaching and faith, but a cause and effect relationship. Yes, your faith is inherently connected to the preaching. When God desired to mobilize faith, He sent a preacher. As I direct your attention to the impotence of preaching, realize that impotency in our preaching produces impotency in our faith.

Chapter 1

CAN WE ALL GET ALONG?

ON MARCH 3, 1991, MEMBERS OF THE LOS ANGELES Police Department approached Rodney King and two passengers as they drove west on the Foothill Freeway. After a high-speed chase, King was apprehended, tackled, tased, and viciously beaten with clubs by four LAPD officers. George Holliday captured much of the fracas on a camcorder from his apartment window. Major news networks provided extensive footage of King being beaten by police officers while lying on the ground. Subsequently, the Los Angeles District Attorney charged four officers with assault and three of the four with the use of excessive force.

On April 29, 1992, because the non-black jury could not agree on a verdict, they acquitted three of the officers and could not agree about one of the charges for the fourth. The evening after the verdict, riots erupted and peaked in intensity over the next two days. Fifty-three lives were lost and more than 2,000 people were injured. Material losses were estimated between $800 million and $1 billion.

Do you remember the plaintive call of Rodney King as he sought to squelch the rioting and looting? Although he had been the victim, in responding to the tragedy of the riots, King cried out, "Can we all get along?"

Some have argued that the reason we cannot get along is based in part on our brain. I beg to differ. The reason we cannot get along is based totally on our heart. The heart of the human problem is the problem of the human heart. The problem of the human heart is sin. Sin and its residual effects continually plague all human relationships. Sin plagues us economically, legally, physically, physiologically, psychologically, and yes, even sociologically.

No person desires to have a toothache. However, a severe toothache is not an insurmountable problem if we know that pulling the tooth or filling the cavity will eliminate the pain. As painful as the toothache may be, the solution is only a dentist's visit away.

Likewise, no person should prefer sin. Certainly, our Lord prefers that we never ever sin, not even one time.

"But immorality or any impurity or greed must not even be named among you, as is proper among saints" (Ephesians 5:3). However, sin should not paralyze us individually nor paralyze the collective pursuits of our fellowship. Instead, sin should mobilize us. Sin should become an occasion for us to graciously override the residual ills of immorality. Individuals and churches must become able and remain willing to work toward overcoming sin in the lives of each of its members. "And if one member suffers, all the members suffer with it" (1 Corinthians 12:26).

Through Jesus Christ, God has given us His objective. Therefore, the church's supreme objective and our own should be to help sinners overcome their sin problem. Then and only then can saints glorify God as they ought. God not only deserves His glory, but He wants His glory. Thus, He has provided the process by which believers can overcome the sin problem that disrupts harmony between believers.

 What is allowing the derailment of God's supreme agenda?

THE INDICTMENT

I promised you that I would be a Nehemiah and see both the mess that we are in and also speak the message that I believe will lead us out of this mess. I promised to speak the truth to you, at whatever cost. I believe that our fellowship within the church systematically fails. Our response is often not only unspiritual, but even anti-spiritual, being totally inconsistent with principles from Scripture. Often, our response conflicts with the example of Jesus. Yes, our wrong responses to sin and to saints who sin cause more casualties than the already committed sin. Therefore, the church needs to subscribe to a biblical sociology so that it can think like God and act like Jesus. We need to think like God and respond like Jesus in our reaction to sin and those who sin. How did Jesus respond to sin and those who sinned? We shall later see!

What is allowing the derailment of God's supreme agenda? The preaching has always been at the heart of God's promotion process. Notice that I said the preaching. Naturally, you cannot have preaching without the preacher. We will take up the matter of the preacher on another occasion. The preacher then becomes God's man. Even though he, himself, often is bleeding while leading, he is still God's man.

Whenever God wanted to initiate a major paradigm shift among His people, He sent a preaching prophet. He intended for the preaching and teaching of His Word to move His people. By design, preaching should bring about immediate and radical changes within people.

Jonah came preaching (see Matthew 12:41). Through preaching, John the Baptist introduced Jesus and ushered the ministry of Jesus into the world (see Matthew 3:1-12, John 1:19-37). Jesus Christ, Himself came preaching (see Mark 1:14). The former demoniac went about preaching (see Mark 5:20). On the first Pentecost after the resurrection of Jesus, the apostle Peter, through preaching, sliced murder right out of the hearts of those who had crucified Jesus (see Acts 2:36-42). Philip the evangelist went about preaching (see Acts 8:12). Preaching pricked hearts and set the stage for radical and revolutionary changes within and among the people of God. Even now, the preaching of the Word should prick hearts.

The Principle Preached

I am not opposed to the preaching of "how-to" sermons. I also believe that doing nothing but condemning people with hellfire-and-brimstone sermons is of little redemptive value. Sermons that teach us how to do what we should do are among my favorites. Please, however, allow me to ask a question: "What does the sermon teach us to do?" If our sermons are not affecting hearts as sermons once did, what has changed? If sermons are not continuing to cause paradigm shifts toward mature spirituality, what has happened? How did it happen? When did it happen? Why did it happen? Better yet, what will be done to restore the health of preaching? The adversary has thrown us a curve. We swung and thought we hit it, but we really missed.

Notice the components of the apostolic preaching that radically changed the world. With God's approval, Jesus preached and prayed for unity. Jesus preached the principle of oneness: "I have other sheep, which are not of this fold; I must bring them also, and they will hear My voice; and they will become one flock with one shepherd" (John 10:16). He even prayed for the principle of unity:

"I do not ask on behalf of these alone, but for those also who believe in Me through their word; that they may all be one; even as You, Father, are in Me and I in You, that they also may be in Us, so that the world may believe that You sent Me" (John 17:20-21). Obviously, unity was and even now is a God idea.

The apostle Peter preached the principle of oneness in Christ:

> "And it shall be in the last days," God says, "that I will pour forth of my Spirit on all mankind; and your sons and your daughters shall prophesy, and your young men shall see visions, and your old men shall dream dreams;...and it shall be that everyone who calls on the name of the Lord will be saved...For the promise is for you and your children and for all who are far off, as many as the Lord our God will call to Himself" (Acts 2:17, 21, 39).

Did you notice the oneness, all mankind, everyone who calls and all who are far off? That oneness placed salvation on the sovereignty of God. It allowed Him the privilege of deciding who would participate in His privileges. That message of oneness potentially welcomed both Jew and Gentiles into the body of Christ. Although Peter preached the principle of oneness (see Acts 2), it was many years later before Gentiles were, in reality, welcomed into that oneness within the body of Christ (see Acts 10). Indeed, oneness was a God idea. Why the delay?

THE PRACTICE PREACHED

Although Peter had preached the principle of oneness, the church had not yet begun to participate in that oneness. Why? As of yet, Peter had not preached the practice that would have implemented the principle of his preaching. The preaching of only the principle does not fully change human behavior. It is the preaching of the practice that implements the principle that brings about the complete change.

Observe the elements of his preaching (see Acts chapters 10-11). First, he implemented a practice that honored the principle—he went to the home of a Gentile:

> When Peter entered, Cornelius met him, and fell at his feet and worshiped him. But Peter raised him up, saying, "Stand up; I too am just a man." As he talked with him, he entered and found many people assembled. And he said to them, "You yourselves know how unlawful it is for a man who is a Jew to associate with a foreigner or to visit him; and yet God has shown me that I should not call any man unholy or unclean" (Acts 10:25-28).

He did not consult with the apostles, nor did he consult with any other leaders in Jerusalem. He just launched out obeying God Himself.

Second, after following a practice that honored the principle, he then preached Jesus, the principle of oneness:

"Opening his mouth, Peter said: 'I most certainly understand now that God is not one to show partiality, but in every nation the man who fears Him and does what is right is welcome to Him'" (Acts 10:34-35).

What do I mean by preaching the principle? To preach the principle is to expound on the core truth or the essence of the matter. Simply preaching the principle falls short of recommending a specific manner in which the principle may be implemented. When we only preach the principle, we do not teach people *how* to do what we are telling them they should do.

Preaching only the principle, however, insignificantly changes human behavior. Therefore, in addition to preaching the principle, he preached the practice that implemented the principle: "Surely no one can refuse the water for these to be baptized who have received the Holy Spirit just as we did, can he? And he ordered them to be baptized in the name of Jesus Christ. Then they asked him to stay on for a few days" (Acts 10:47-48).

In addition to preaching the principle, we must preach the practice that applies the principle, for until we preach the practice that applies the principle, nothing changes. When the apostle Peter preached the practice, it immediately caused circumcised Jewish believers who had gone with Peter to Caesarea to baptize uncircumcised Gentile believers (see Acts 10:44-48). Preaching immediately caused circumcised Jewish believers who had not gone with Peter to Caesarea to accept the uncircumcised Gentile believers (see

Acts 11:1-18). Baptizing and accepting Gentiles into fellowship with Jewish believers indicated a radical philosophical and sociological change.

> Peter preached both the principle and the practice. He did so without obtaining prior approval from anyone except God.

Until Peter preached the engaging practice that applied the principle of oneness, both Jews and Gentiles remained separate. Not only did they remain separated, but they also remained segregated. The unity for which Jesus had prayed and about which Peter had preached did not become a reality until the practice of the principle was preached.

What practice did Peter preach? He preached the practice of an integration of socialization with the Gentiles. Peter preached the very practice that Jesus modeled when He offered to place His lips on the same drinking container in which the Samaritan woman placed her lips (see John 4:7). Peter went to the home of a Gentile and ate with him: "You went to uncircumcised men and ate with them" (Acts 11:3). Also, he preached the practice of baptism that upheld the principle of oneness.

Peter preached both the principle and the practice. He did so without obtaining prior approval from anyone except God. In fact, the leaders took issue with the practice. When Peter came up to Jerusalem, they confronted him about practicing the principle. "And when Peter came up to Jerusalem, those who were circumcised took issue with him, saying, 'You went to uncircumcised men and ate with them'" (Acts 11:2-3). How interesting it is to note that those in Jerusalem raised no concerns when he had earlier preached the principle of oneness: "For the promise is for you and your children and for all who are far off, as many as the Lord our God will call to Himself" (Acts 2:39). Rather, they synchronized their voices and echoed the same sentiments. After he preached (applied) the practice, however, all hell broke loose. Opposition surfaced not from preaching the principle, but from preaching (implementing) the practice.

Throughout human history, God has radically changed the world through the preaching of one man. Not once did God ever require His preacher to consult with the establishment before preaching. Nor did He *allow* him to do so.

For I would have you know, brethren, that the gospel which was preached by me is not according to man. For I neither received it from man, nor was I taught it, but I received it through a revelation of Jesus Christ. For you have heard of my former manner of life in Judaism, how I used to persecute the church of God beyond measure and tried to destroy it; and I was advancing in Judaism beyond many of my contemporaries among my countrymen, being more extremely zealous for my ancestral traditions. But when God, who had set me apart even from my mother's womb and called me through His grace, was pleased to reveal His Son in me so that I might preach Him among the Gentiles, I did not immediately consult with flesh and blood, nor did I go up to Jerusalem to those who were apostles before me; but I went away to Arabia, and returned once more to Damascus (Galatians 1:11-17).

Neither did God require His preaching man to consult with the establishment before preaching the practice that applies the principle. When the apostle Paul received his preaching assignment, he did not consult with the establishment, but rather he went about preaching what radically changed human history (see Galatians 1:11-24). He knew that to preach what pleased the establishment would be to preach what displeased God. "For am I now seeking the favor of men, or of God? Or am I striving to please men? If I was still trying to please men, I would not be a bond-servant of Christ" (Galatians 1:10). He did not consult with the establishment before he preached the principle nor before he preached the practice.

Now you might be thinking, "What does this have to do with the impotence of our preaching?" Keep reading with unbiased eyes. Examine my case thoroughly with an objective mind. Let the facts speak. President Ronald Reagan spoke a characteristic truth when he quoted President John Adams: "Facts are stubborn things." The Great Communicator also spoke a challenging truth when he said, "Don't be afraid to see what you see."

Chapter 2

WE MUST PREACH THE PRINCIPLE

E WHO PREACH MUST PREACH THE PRINCIPLE. We have God-given authority and a mandate from Heaven to preach the principle. No one who claims to understand the Word would disagree. In unison we declare that we have a mandate to preach the Word without apology.

> *I solemnly charge you in the presence of God and of Christ Jesus, who is to judge the living and the dead, and by His appearing and His kingdom: preach the word; be ready in season and out of season; reprove, rebuke,*

exhort, with great patience and instruction. For the time will come when they will not endure sound doctrine; but wanting to have their ears tickled, they will accumulate for themselves teachers in accordance to their own desires, and will turn away their ears from the truth and will turn aside to myths (2 Timothy 4:1-4).

There in the context lies a warning. The time will come when those who once had embraced truth will decide they have already embraced enough truth. These will, therefore, turn their ears away from hearing further truth. In other words, these will say, "I have changed enough. Preach no more change sermons."

Who are those who will turn away their ears? Leaders among the believers are those who will turn away. Those who turn away will accumulate for themselves teachers. The establishment, the hierarchy, and the leaders will restrict and prohibit the preaching. How sad! We, ourselves, are not to be alarmed. The apostle Paul warned of such devastation. He saw it coming. He saw how the elders of the church would form an authoritative hierarchy and rape the preaching of its power. In his solemn warning to the elders of the church, he prophesied this truth: "And from among your own selves men will arise, speaking perverse things, to draw away the disciples after them" (Acts 20:30).

WE MUST PREACH THE PRACTICE

With equal power we must also preach the practice that applies and implements the principle. Herein, however, lies our paramount problem. Our system, which produces the team concept of leadership consisting of elders, deacons, and ministers, is an unbalanced one. Regardless of how loudly we declare team cooperation, you and I both know that the elders exercise executive override privileges. Without recourse, they can veto any and all practices offered by the preaching and by the preachers who preach.

> We must never, even with all our good intentions, allow the divine channel of implementing the preached principles to become hijacked by human leadership.

Our system readily applauds preachers for preaching the principle, but regularly apprehends us for preaching the practice that upholds the principle. Yes, our system allows us to study the principle and preach it, but coerces us to discuss the practice before preaching it. In other words, preach truth, but do not initiate change until the leadership (elders) approves it.

On the surface, it may seem that this is a stroke of wisdom. Yes, some declare that we must place within the system safe-guards to prevent unscrupulous preachers from hijacking the church. God, however, has provided other remedies for that problem. Therefore, we must never, even with all our good intentions, allow the divine channel of implementing the preached principles to become hijacked by human leadership. What safeguards did God put in place to prohibit Moses from leading His people astray? What safeguards did God put in place to keep Timothy from leading His people astray? Are we wiser than God? For them, God placed into the hands of one man the responsibility of preaching both the principle and the practice.

Our preaching of the principle lies impotent because we dare not preach the practice without prior approval from the hierarchy of our establishment. Unfortunately, approval for radical changes rarely comes. First, under cover of expediency, and finally, under command of the authority of executive override, the practice lay dormant far too long.

WHEN WE PREACH THE PRINCIPLE
BUT NOT THE PRACTICE

Let us look at the example of racial reconciliation. What happens when we preach the principle of racial reconciliation but do not preach the practice that implements the principle? No doubt every Holy Spirit-influenced culture opposes racism and racist attitudes within the church. For years, they have preached against the ungodliness of segregation. Most every attendee of every church has heard at least one sermon condemning racial segregation. Why then is 11:00 a.m. on Sunday still the most segregated hour in America? I believe that we have made so little progress in race relations because we preach the principle of racial reconciliation, but not the practice of racial reconciliation. Let me illustrate why with this example from my own personal experience.

In the summer of 1995, a Caucasian preacher and I participated in a race-relations symposium in Raleigh, North Carolina. Several years afterwards, he relocated near Atlanta to serve another congregation. Several years after moving, he asked me if I would speak to his new congregation on the subject of racism within the church. I agreed to speak on this one condition: that he and his elders (leaders) would meet with me and the elders of the church where I preached and discuss ways to practice the principles that would bring about more social fellowship between the two congregations. He emphatically said, "My elders are not there yet. I need you to come and speak and help me to get them there." Intensely, we contrasted his proposal with my request. After he was unable to move me from my stubborn position, he dejectedly said, "I will call you back."

A few days later at 9:30 p.m., when he knew I would not be in the office, he called and left a voice message retracting his invitation. I believe that this brother sincerely wanted to effect positive change and was very disillusioned with his leaders. Therefore, I was not surprised when six weeks later he took a preaching position at another congregation and moved 800 miles away.

Imagine that: Two preachers, black and white, who desired to foster a fellowship relationship between their respective congregations. Unfortunately, our hands were tied due to the stubbornness of the team leaders (elders). The elders of the church where I was preaching would have readily welcomed fellowship with our Caucasian brothers and sisters in Christ. Usually, we are more receptive of them than they are of us, sometimes even to our own personal and institutional demise.

How sad it is when you cannot get church leaders to even discuss practicing the principles that have been preached. How sad it is that the preaching of the practice must wait behind the approval of the hierarchy. God never intended for it to be that way.

What in the world are we preaching for? That preacher and I both could preach principles without prior approval and without any opposition, but neither of us could preach the practice of the principles of unity that would eliminate racism—without prior approval. Why would the preacher even need the elders' approval to engage congregations into a fellowship relationship? He wielded the authority to preach the principles that would eliminate racism, yet he was withheld from preaching the practice that would activate the principles. Frequently, leadership handcuffs the preaching to the podium.

Now lest you think this is indicative of only an ungodly leadership, consider this. In March 2000 during his Sunday morning sermon, a preacher I know quite well expounded and explained the great commission passages of Matthew 28:16-20. He emphasized that making disciples is the primary responsibility of the saints of God. He even went so far as to say that mature disciples make and mature other disciples so that they, too, would make and mature other disciples. He specifically stated that every disciple has the responsibility of leading people to follow Jesus. To that great expository preaching, the whole church shouted a resounding "Amen!"

Time and time again he emphasized that evangelism must always be the church's primary purpose. To that, the congregation again shouted a resounding "Amen!"

He talked about how Jesus entrusted the gospel to the hands of a dozen itinerant preachers and they went about turning the world upside down. To that, they all shouted a resounding "Amen!"

Near the end of that often amen-interrupted sermon, he shared a practice that would uphold the principles he had just preached. He shared with the congregation how he could preach the gospel to the multitudes through a national television program. This national medium could help them to accomplish their priority purpose more efficiently and effectively than any other. Then he asked for a commitment from the members who would be willing to financially support that endeavor. To that, the church echoed a resounding "Amen!" and instantly committed more than 50 percent of the necessary funds.

Although the people enthusiastically responded, there was a problem. The preacher had not previously consulted with the elders (the hierarchy) of the congregation. The elders exercised their executive override and vetoed the effort. They vehemently objected because he had not received approval from them first. He could preach the principle without prior approval, but dared not preach the practice without prior approval.

Some five years later, those elders were still badgering the preacher for having preached the practice without first having obtaining their approval. They never ever let that preacher forget that he had "gone to the church without first coming to them."

No wonder the preaching of the gospel infrequently changes the lives of listeners. We can preach the principles at will, but we are not allowed to preach the practice that upholds the principles unless we obtain prior permission. To the preaching of the principles, the leaders all shouted "Amen!" To the preaching of the practice that promotes the principles, the leaders shouted "Oh, no!"

This is not a criticism of godly leaders (elders). This is not even a criticism of ungodly leaders. They are not to blame. Blame serves no useful purpose. Correction is the only redemptive issue at hand. This is a call for a critique of our establishment's system of hierarchy—for a flawed thread has woven itself into the very fabric of the design of our leadership system. Yes, I place full blame on the design of our leadership system.

Years ago, I heard the trumpeting voice of Dr. Eugene Lawton passionately declaring that we might have to surrender the facets of this world to follow the course of its choosing, but when it comes to the will of God we ought to "let the church be the church!" It is time again for this clarion call: Let the church be the church! For this to happen, the preacher must exercise not only unrestricted and unrestrained authority to preach the principles, but also to preach the practice that implements the preached principles. Otherwise, our preaching becomes reduced to a mere suggestion session on Sunday.

I am well aware that these pointed statements run the risk of raising stern critics. After I have been beaten by my critics, hopefully, I can muster enough energy to raise my begging, bloodied brow and cry, "Can we all get along?" Until then, read, take your seat, and await your turn to throw your stone. Save some energy; there will be more truth in subsequent chapters that may make you want to throw additional stones.

REFLECTIONS

List seven renovating principles that you have heard preached within your place of worship. By "renovating," I mean outline a specific course of action that significantly brought your life into a greater harmony with the will of God.

1. _____

2. _____

3. _____

4. _____

5. _____

6. _____

7. _____

Was the practice of those principles preached and implemented? If so, shout, "Amen!" and list how. If not, why do you
think the practice was not also preached?

_____

_____

_____

_____

_____

_____

List several principles you have heard preached for which
no practice has ever been implemented.

_____

_____

_____

_____

_____

_____

Discuss the pros and cons of removing the preaching of the practice from the approval of the hierarchy.

_____

_____

_____

_____

_____

_____

_____

_____

_____

Chapter 3

CAN WE GET ALONG WITH SAINTS WHO SIN?

F YOU HAVE GREAT DIFFICULTY ADOPTING GOD'S mandate for getting along with saints who sin, it is because you have failed to internalize a proper practice. If you have not internalized a proper practice, then why have you not? Could it be that you heard the principle preached, but the practice was withheld? So that you will not throw all your stones, sit back, relax, take a deep breath, and proceed cautiously.

When all is said and done, the church's number one responsibility to sinners is to help them overcome the penalty of sin.

As sinners are born again, they become saints because they have thus overcome the ***penalty*** of sin. The church's number one responsibility to saints is to help them to overcome the ***practice*** of sin so that they can ultimately live eternally away from the ***presence*** of sin. Preaching is all about the sin problem. Therefore, we must preach both the principle and the practice, which helps saints overcome their sin problem.

Too often, our leadership system renders our preaching impotent. Impotent preaching renders individuals and congregations unaware, unable, unavailable, and unwilling to help unbelievers and believers overcome their sin problem.

What Is Sin?

Sin is the intentional and/or unintentional positioning of one's heart in opposition to God (see Matthew 15:18-20). When our heart opposes what God approves, we become guilty of sin (see Acts 10:13-15). When our heart approves what God opposes, we become guilty of sin (see Acts 5:1-4, 8:18-22).

Sin surfaces when the human heart favorably accepts what God rejects. Long ago, Jesus declared that sin erupts from within the human heart. When He explained a parable, He taught that the things that defile a person come from within the heart of that person:

> *"But the things that proceed out of the mouth come from the heart, and those defile the man. For out of the heart come evil thoughts, murders, adulteries, fornications, thefts, false witness, slanders. These are the things which*

defile the man; but to eat with unwashed hands does not defile the man" (Matthew 15:18-20).

God holds us accountable for what our heart favors and/or rejects. Occasionally, we may sin, yet be unaware of our sin. Yes, we may sin unknowingly. Yes, our disposition of heart bears the blame. God charges us with guilt when our heart opposes Him. Sin starts with the disposition of our heart, not just with the direction of our behavior.

THE HUMAN HEART OPPOSES
WHAT HEAVEN APPROVES

When our heart opposes what God approves, we become guilty of sin. God wanted to place His divine favor upon the people of Nineveh. For His full favor to flow, the people of Nineveh needed to repent of their wickedness. Therefore, God wanted Jonah to preach to them so that they might turn to Him. Jonah, however, did not want the favor of God to reign upon the people of Nineveh, so he adamantly refused to go and preach to them.

The word of the Lord came to Jonah the son of Amittai saying, "Arise, go to Nineveh the great city and cry against it, for their wickedness has come up before Me." But Jonah rose up to flee to Tarshish from the presence of the Lord. So he went down to Joppa, found a ship which was going to Tarshish, paid the fare and went down into it to go with them to Tarshish from the presence of the Lord (Jonah 1:1-3).

Even before Jonah began to flee, however, his heart opposed God. From that moment he became guilty of sin. God decided that through Jesus Christ He would invite all mankind to sit at the fraternal table of brotherhood within His Kingdom. From the day of Pentecost, the apostles began to preach the gospel of inclusion. Unfortunately, they failed to understand the full essence of the gospel of inclusion and therefore, were very negligent in practicing it. When the time came, God singled out the apostle Peter to bring into practice what they had been preaching. What may have appeared to some to be mere incidentals were really not incidentals at all. God orchestrated the timing of hunger with Peter's regularly scheduled prayer session (see Acts 10:1-12).

Through this experience, God provided a vision to Peter to persuade him to welcome the Gentiles into the kingdom of God. He gave Peter a vision of the sky opening up and a sheet descending to earth that contained all kinds of four-footed animals, crawling creatures of the earth, and birds of the air. Within the vision, He said to Peter, "Get up...kill and eat" (Acts 10:13). Initially, Peter refused the divine command of God. Peter proudly exclaimed his dietary innocence declaring that he had never eaten anything unholy and unclean (see Acts 10:14). At that moment, his heart opposed what God approved (see Acts 10:13-15). Indeed, God approved of his eating; otherwise God would have never commanded.

THE HUMAN HEART APPROVES
WHAT HEAVEN OPPOSES

When our heart approves what God opposes, we become guilty of sin. From the beginning, God provided for His people (see Genesis 2:8-9). He conditioned the heart of His people to take care of each other's needs. Subsequently, from the church's beginning days in Jerusalem, His people provided for the necessities of each other within their community (see Acts 2:44-45). God approved of selling one's property and donating all the proceeds to the church. Many believers sold and donated with God's approval.

 On a crowded day at the mall, you might catch a glimpse of a $50 bill dangling out of a woman's purse as she casually strolls through the aisles.

Ananias and Sapphira sold property and conceived within their hearts to lie about how much they received from the sale (see Acts 5:1-11). Within their hearts, they approved of lying about the sale price. At that moment, their heart favored what God opposed. God opposed lying; therefore, they became guilty of sin because their hearts approved what God opposed. To show His disgust with lying, God reduced their bodies to room temperature and young morticians placed them together in the cemetery.

Simon, the former deceiving so-called magic man, wanted to experience the apostolic gift of the Holy Spirit. He offered money to the apostles so that he, too, might possess that great power. God opposed the very notion that His gifts could be bought with money. In that instance, Simon's heart approved what God opposed. Therefore, the apostles rebuked him for his sinful desire (see Acts 8:18-22). Yes, he found himself in the gall of sin, hosting a heart that opposed God.

On a crowded day at the mall, you might catch a glimpse of a $50 bill dangling out of a woman's purse as she casually strolls through the aisles. Quickly your thoughts fast forward to a delicious meal at Outback Steak House. Delicious and free, you think. So, you decide to swipe the $50 bill and stash it away for the evening's meal. You sheepishly glance around to see who is watching. You cautiously move closer, but just at that instant the woman looks at her purse, pushes the money out of sight into the purse, and briskly walks away. You never get the opportunity to place your sticky fingers on the money. Dejectedly, you limp out of the mall toward home and your cold bologna sandwich for the evening. God still charges your heart with thievery.

In all matters, God assigns to us the intentions of our heart. Yes, you are a thief. God assigns to our heart all the wrong that we favor doing. Yes, He assigns to us the wrong that we favor doing that we never ever do. At first this may seem like a rotten deal, but consider this. God also assigns to us all the good that we favor doing. Yes, He assigns to us the good that we favor doing that we never actually do. My,

Lord, what a gracious deal! Occasionally, we would do good but are hindered beyond by factors and forces beyond our control. God credits our account anyway. God knew that you would have gone to the hospital to visit the sick, but your employer needed overtime hours from you. Praise the Lord for a gracious God like this. You are rewarded for all the good that you would have done but were hindered from doing. God adds the credits to your reward account. Now that is a good deal!

THE PRINCIPLE OF SIN

Can we really get along with saints who sin? That is ridiculous, you say. Jesus came to do away with sin. How in the world could we ever think we should get along with those who sin? Are they not in direct opposition to God? That seemed to be the Jews' thought process until the apostle Paul issued his blanket indictment: "For all have sinned and fall short of the glory of God" (Romans 3:23). Notice that he said, "All," not "Y'all." Sometimes we behave more like Satan than like our Savior.

Adam and Eve declared their independence from God. They attempted to live independently of the instructions that God had given unto them. Attempting to live independently of God, introduced sin into the human world. "Therefore, just as through one man, sin entered into the world, and death through sin, and so death spread to all men, because all sinned" (Romans 5:12). Ever since Adam introduced sin into the human race, it has woven itself into the very fabric of human existence. Everyone has experienced sin. "For all have sinned and fall short of the glory of God" (Romans 3:23).

There exists a permeating principle of sin: "If we say that we have no sin, we are deceiving ourselves and the truth is not in us" (1 John 1:8). There exists within us a sin nature (see Ephesians 2:3). When the word *sin* is singular, it usually refers to the nature rather than the number of sins committed. For that permeating principle of sin, there comes a past penalty for sins (see Romans 6:23). Separation and eternal isolation from the dominance of God is the past penalty for sin (see 2 Thessalonians 1:7-10). Also, for that permeating principle of sin there is a present power of sin (see Romans 6:16-20), which forever plagues us (see Romans 7:23-25).

The Preference for Sin

There exists a possible preference to sin. "My little children, I am writing these things to you so that you may not sin. And if anyone sins, we have an Advocate with the Father, Jesus Christ the righteous" (1 John 2:1). We do not have to sin. God reminds us that we are never tempted with temptations that are beyond our capability to resist.

> *No temptation has overtaken you but such as is common to man; and God is faithful, who will not allow you to be tempted beyond what you are able, but with the temptation will provide the way of escape also, so that you will be able to endure it (1 Corinthians 10:13).*

Obviously, we can control our bodies because He charges us to withhold our bodies from sin (see Romans 6:13-14). No, we do not have to sin, but we probably will sin.

Since we must continually make decisions, we often make wrong decisions. Because we possess such a strong inclination to sin, we make decisions that are anti-scriptural. Being ignorant, we often fail to resist sin. Out of ignorance, religious people murdered Jesus (see Acts 3:14-17). Out of ignorance, some refused to subject themselves to the righteousness of God (see Romans 10:3). Being rebellious, we often fail to resist sin (see Romans 1:18-25, Jude 11).

THE PROPITIATION FOR SIN

There exists a powerful propitiation for our sin. "And He Himself is the propitiation for our sins; and not for ours only, but also for those of the whole world" (1 John 2:2). Jesus is the propitiation (adequate satisfaction) for our sin. Our good deeds are not the satisfaction. Jesus has already satisfied God's righteous demand for our sin. God will not and cannot tolerate sin. Someone had to pay the penalty. Jesus died on the cross, paying the sin-price for us (see Ephesians 2:16, Colossians 1:20).

Since Jesus is the propitiation for our sins, we have no reason to deny sin that is within our lives. "If we say that we have not sinned, we make Him a liar and His word is not in us" (1 John 1:10). The basic human problem persists because we keep disagreeing with God. We disagree with God that sin is present and also how to purge it. We call it an accident, but God calls it an abomination. We call it a fascination, but God calls it a fatality. We call it liberty, but God calls it lawlessness.

Jesus is the propitiation for sins; therefore, we must confess it (see 1 John 1:8-9). Confess means to speak the same thing as another. When we sin, God holds the charge of guilt against us. We must say about ourselves what God says about ourselves. God says that we are guilty, so we must therefore say, "Yes, God, I am guilty" (see Psalm 32). However, be reminded that divine forgiveness is divine forgetfulness (see Hebrews 10:17).

The concept of propitiation, or adequate satisfaction for sin, is well illustrated by the story of the congregation of Israel murmuring against Moses and Aaron:

> But on the next day all the congregation of the sons of Israel grumbled against Moses and Aaron, saying, "You are the ones who have caused the death of the Lord's people." It came about, however, when the congregation had assembled against Moses and Aaron, that they turned toward the tent of meeting, and behold, the cloud covered it and the glory of the Lord appeared. Then Moses and Aaron came to the front of the tent of meeting, and the Lord spoke to Moses, saying, "Get away from among this congregation, that I may consume them instantly." Then they fell on their faces. Moses said to Aaron, "Take your censer and put in it fire from the altar, and lay incense on it; then bring it quickly to the congregation and make atonement for them, for wrath has gone forth

from the Lord, the plague has begun!" Then Aaron took it as Moses had spoken, and ran into the midst of the assembly, for behold, the plague had begun among the people. So he put on the incense and made atonement for the people. He took his stand between the dead and the living, so that the plague was checked (Numbers 16:41-48).

Did you notice how the people complained against Moses and Aaron, charging them with causing the death of the people of God? Arrogantly they assembled against Moses and Aaron at the tent of meeting. This confrontation angered God Almighty till He decided to destroy their adversaries. Instantly, God went about destroying the rebels, but Moses sent Aaron into the midst of the assembly with a censer of incense, making atonement for the rebellious people. His intercessory response proved to be an adequate satisfaction or appeasement to God for their sin. Due to this satisfaction, God restrained His destroying hand after killing only 14,700 people—a small percentage of the total population.

What stopped more people from dying? The intercessory intervention of Aaron satisfied God. Because Jesus is our propitiation for sin, no one has to die the second death (see Revelation 20:14-15). Through the sacrificial death of Jesus, God has satisfied His own righteous demand for justice. Indeed, Jesus is our propitiation: He is our adequate satisfaction for sin.

Chapter 4

GOD'S REMEDY FOR SIN

THE APOSTLE JOHN EMPHASIZED THE PERSONAL reality of sin (see 1 John 1:8, 10). In that same chapter, the Holy Spirit of God indicts all human beings as having become guilty of sin. He goes so far as to say that when we say we have not sinned, it is equivalent to making God a liar. Using the present tense, "We have," the Holy Spirit of God informed believers of the functional role of Jesus: "My little children, I am writing these things to you so that you may not sin. And if anyone sins, we have an Advocate with the Father, Jesus Christ the righteous" (1 John 2:1).

Because Jesus is righteous, He is our advocate with the Father. As our advocate, He is our face-to-face counselor for the defense. Therein, He continually pleads to our Father on our behalf. As our counselor for the defense, Jesus translates and transmits our human concerns to the divine father. Also, because Jesus is righteous, He is our propitiation for sin. As our propitiation, He is our adequate satisfaction for all our sin. Now you can see why only Jesus can be the solution for our sin problem. All of us have a sin problem and need God's sin solution. How does He solve our sin problem? Let us consider God's remedy for sin.

1. **Law.** The first portion of God's remedy to sin is law: "So that you may not sin" (1 John 2:1). Do not sin. Law deals with the prohibition and prevention relative to the practice of sin. First and foremost, God challenges us to live above the principle and practice of sin. Take some time and observe closely how prohibitive in nature the Ten Commandments are.

2. **Grace.** The second portion of God's remedy for sin is grace: "And if anyone sins" (1 John 2:1b-2). When believers sin, we apply grace. Grace deals with remediation and rehabilitation relative to the penalty of sin. Grace is unmerited favor and acceptance with God. Through our sins we became undeserving people, yet through His grace, He has accepted us and

approved of us. Because of the kindness of His grace, He gives us what we do not deserve: forgiveness of sins. Grace allows us to receive what God provides. It is our license to receive grace. It is our license to receive of the wealth of our spiritual inheritance. Grace is the reason for our faith. It is the alpha, the beginning of our faith. Even the opportunity to develop faith in God is a gift of God (see Ephesians 2:8).

Time and time again through Jesus, God applied both law and grace to each instance of sin. Guilty prosecutors caught a woman in the very act of adultery (see John 8:1-10). These students of the law ushered her out of the presence of her lover and into the presence of her Lord. The prosecuting professors presented a pop quiz to the master Teacher. First, they reminded Him of their interpretation of the Law, and second, they demanded His application of the law.

First, Jesus confronted them with law. "He who is without sin among you, let him be the first to throw a stone at her" (John 8:7). The law required the witness to cast the first stone (see Deuteronomy 17:7), but the Law also called for stoning both the man and the woman (see Deuteronomy 22:22-24). After the pseudo-scholars snuck away, Jesus turned His attention to the woman. He showed her both with grace ("I do not condemn you") and law ("From now on sin no more") (John 8:11). Then Jesus released the woman to live out her years in peace. Hallelujah!

Jesus is our only solution for sin. Peace is His
profession.

We must always apply both portions of the remedy for
each sin. We must always apply both law and grace. This
must be our order of response whether within our personal
life or within the corporate life of the church. Unfortunately,
some are law-oriented only, while others are grace-oriented
only. How sad!

Too often, we apply only law to those we do not like, while
we seek to apply only grace to those we like. Yes, we sinfully
subscribe to the slogan, "Law toward your children but grace
toward mine." We do not have the right to abuse our liberty
in such inconsistent manner. Kingdom principles must be
honored as such. Therefore, in every instance of sin we must
apply both law and grace. Law caused God to destroy 14,700
people, but grace caused Him to honor Aaron's sacrifice and
stop the plague (see Numbers 16:41-48).

THE PEACE OF SIN

Indeed, Jesus is our only solution for sin. Peace is His
profession. "For He Himself is our peace, who made both
groups into one and broke down the barrier of the dividing
wall" (Ephesians 2:14). Peace is His production. "By abol-
ishing in His flesh the enmity, which is the Law of commandments contained in ordinances, so that in Himself He might
make the two into one new man, thus establishing peace"

(Ephesians 2:15). And peace is also His proclamation. "And he came and preached peace to you who were far away, and peace to those who were near" (Ephesians 2:17). Regardless of His audience, Jesus preached His one sermon: peace (see Acts 10:36).

Peace is the absence of the distresses that are caused by sin. Jesus was always preaching to help people sustain relations that were free of the distresses that are caused by sin. Jesus orders us to tell the truth. Why? If we lie, we will distress relationships. He orders us not to steal. Why? If we steal, we will create distress in our relationships.

Because of personal differences, our relationships will never be 100 percent distress free. They, however, can be relatively free of the distresses that are caused by sin. For example, if I prefer to eat at Wendy's while you prefer to eat at McDonald's, some stress might surface as we attempt to juggle our schedule to accommodate both preferences. Peace demands that we obtain our food without creating distresses from sin. Therefore, we must decide how to proceed without sin. In order to keep the peace, we must keep sin out of the equation.

Peace is restored favor and relationship with God. It is the reestablishment and reconciliation of our relationship with God. Peace announces that we have received what God provides. It is our license to relax. It is our license to relax in the confidence of our spiritual inheritance. Peace is the result of our faith. It is the omega, the ending of our faith. When faith is exercised, it produces peace.

The church is the body of Christ. What Jesus did, the church must also do. Jesus was God's chief promoter of peace; therefore the church must be God's chief promoter of peace. Peace must be our individual profession, production, and proclamation. Peace must be the profession of the church, the production of the church, and the proclamation of the church.

Our individual responsibility is to help people to overcome sin. God has assigned to the church exclusively the responsibility of helping people to overcome their sin problem. If the church refuses to accept its exclusive assignment, God has no further need for it. There are entities within our communities that assist with all other human needs. There are, however, no entities that assist with helping people to overcome their sin problem. Throughout the world, the church is to be God's chief promoter of the peace process. Therefore we can never become too ashamed to help.

This is the exclusive assignment that God has given to the church. Unfortunately it is the one assignment that the church is least active in performing

Several years ago a preacher friend and I were riding along Bragg Boulevard on the Ft. Bragg Army base. Bragg Boulevard was rumored to be the strip where prostitutes frequented on GI payday, the first and fifteenth day of every month. Noticing several women of the evening, I kiddingly remarked to my preacher friend, "Let's walk the strip, teach these women about God, and see if we can deter some from this type of lifestyle." Instantly he said, "John, you're crazy. What will people think if they see us out here? I am not going to risk my reputation out here." Although I had initially made the suggestion without any degree of sincerity, his adamant refusal sparked a flint of reality. At the time, my nine-year-old daughter was the sweetest and cutest little thing the world has ever known (even now she is cute and sweet). Later as I reflected upon our conversation I wondered out loud, "My daughter could grow up and wander so far from the Lord until good Christians would not even attempt to persuade her to return to the Lord." How sad! Are we really more concerned about the bad that people will say about us than we are about the good that God will do through us?

You may think despairingly about the potential for success in situations like the one I describe. You may even argue about what is the best winning approach—but please note that Jesus was never so concerned about His reputation that He was unwilling to interact with those whom He wanted to win, regardless of where they had sunk in life.

The church must always be about helping people to over-come sin in their lives. This is the exclusive assignment that God has given to the church. Unfortunately it is the one assignment that the church is least active in performing. Other entities exist to pay utility bills, assist in psychological therapies, and conduct job fairs. I do not say that these good works are off-limits for the church. These good works are not the *priority* unless the church is using them to get at helping people to overcome sin.

If the church neglects to perform its exclusive assignment, of what value is it to God? Imagine rushing a critically ill neighbor to the emergency room at the local hospital. Upon arriving, you notice that the doctors and nurses are manicuring the lawn. You rush inside the hospital and discover it is void of staff members. Quickly, you rush outside and frantically approach the doctors. They inform you that they will be inside once they finish the lawn. When they finally come inside, they say that your neighbor has lost too much blood to recover. What would you think? What value are they to the hospital? Of what value is that staff to the general public or the purpose for which they are ordained? Sure, it is a good thing to manicure the lawn, but manicuring the lawn does not rise to the highest level of priority when lives are in jeopardy.

We can never become too ashamed to help believers overcome sin. Why are we so ashamed when others sin? Are we ashamed because we have not sinned or because we think no one knows about our sins? We have sinned and others do know. That's why the Holy Spirit first removed the cloak from over our sin by declaring that all have been guilty (see 1 John 1:10). One drug addict is not embarrassed to minister to another addict. They know and they know that others know. Therefore, the embarrassment of the guilt factor is non-existent for them. What a challenge for us believers!

Chapter 5

FORGIVENESS IN ACTION

SEVERAL YEARS AGO, GOD GRANTED ME THE privilege of teaching and baptizing Betty (not her real name). Betty had recovered from a twelve-year cocaine addiction. As a matter of fact, she had recovered quite well. At the time, she worked as a registered nurse at the local hospital. Although she had been clean and sober for quite some time, daily she depended upon her meetings with Alcoholics Anonymous and Narcotics Anonymous to remain clean and sober. She invited me to one of their open meetings. I was amazed at how nurturing a room full of former and present addicts could be toward each other. Regardless of what stage of recovery each participant had reached, everyone else provided nurture for improvement. Some even mentioned how they had suffered a relapse. No one offered judgment, just compassionate nurture. I left the meeting understanding why so many, without coercion, attend daily AA meetings, but with coercion we have difficulty getting members to attend weekly church meetings.

When the embarrassment of the guilt factor is alive, we who need help will delay coming forward for help. We will wait until we are faced with a crisis before asking for help. When I have lost my job and am penniless, I will sit in the house until the evictors put my furniture on the street. I insist on subscribing to the bankrupt fake-it-even-though-I-am-not-going-to-make-it syndrome. When I know that grace may be found, however, I will readily come forward. Even when I first receive law, and then grace, I will still come forward. Therefore, believers and the church must establish themselves as being willing to help regardless of the sin. We can never become embarrassed to the extent that we are unwilling to help believers overcome sin.

When you were younger, your mother dressed you in your Sunday best and placed you on the sofa. She issued a strong warning to remain there. You disregarded her warning, went outside, and fell into a puddle of water. How did your mother respond? Was she too embarrassed to help you overcome the dirt? No. She applied law; she spanked you. Then she applied grace; she dressed you in clean clothes. It should be the same within the church. Believers must challenge believers not to sin, but also console them when they do sin.

Which apostle do you think was the worst sinner? This question was on a survey—who do you think most people chose? Most chose Judas. What would you think if I suggested that Peter was equally as bad as Judas? Before you close this book, consider this:

Jesus told Peter that he would deny Him shortly (see Luke 22:34). Peter vehemently denied the Lord (see verses 54-62). Jesus made eye contact with Peter as a nurturing rebuke for his sin. Peter's weeping indicated his heart reaction to his sin. Let us observe the divine response to Peter. After the resurrection, an angel spoke to the women who entered the tomb and told them, "But go, tell His disciples and Peter, 'He is going ahead of you into Galilee; there you will see Him, just as He told you'" (Mark 16:7). By specifically naming Peter, the angel assured that Peter would receive nurture. The angel singled out the very person who had earlier sinned against our Lord. Less than fifty days later, Peter became the chief spokesperson on the day of Pentecost (see Acts 2).

> If Judas had received the nurture that Peter received, likely he would have subsequently behaved differently.

Now let's notice Judas. Judas carried the money bag and had been stealing for a while (see John 12:6). Later, he betrayed Jesus with a kiss. There is no question that Judas' heart was not right, but after he betrayed Jesus, he sought assistance from the chief priest:

> Then when Judas, who had betrayed Him, saw that He had been condemned, he felt remorse and returned the thirty pieces of silver to the chief priests and elders, saying, "I have sinned by betraying innocent blood." But they said, "What is that to us? See to that yourself!" (Matthew 27:3-4).

What was the role of the chief priest? God ordained the chief priest to offer sacrifices for the sins of the people. In other words, the chief priest's main job was to help people to overcome the guilt of sin. Unfortunately, when Judas sought help from him, the chief priest dishonored his office. You know the rest of the story: Judas committed suicide.

Have you ever wondered what might have happened had Judas received adequate nurturing from the chief priest? If Judas had received the nurture that Peter received, likely he would have subsequently behaved differently. If Peter had been treated like Judas, it is likely that he, too, would have behaved differently. When believers are recovering from sin, they do not need less nurturing; they need more nurturing (see Luke chapter 15).

How many people have already jumped off a bridge because we did not help them to overcome the guilt of their sin? They confessed but instead of receiving a helping hand they received negative feedback. When people sin, we need to apply law and say, "Sin no more." We also need to bring them to the recollection of their behavior, but once the person indicates that they are aware of their sin, we must provide grace. People will come for law (discipline) when they are assured of receiving grace also.

Some have erroneously thought that to forgive one must excuse the guilty away from justice. Justice involves future moral accountability. Forgiveness is not excusing the guilty away from justice (see Exodus 22:1, Leviticus 6:1-7, Numbers 5:6-7, 14:18, 2 Samuel 12:6, 9-23, Luke 19:1-10, John 5:1-14, 8:1-10). Forgiveness is revising our thoughtful feelings toward the former guilty one (see Matthew 5:43-48). It is revising our thoughtful behavior toward the former guilty one, wherein we rediscover the humanity of the person who wronged us (see 2 Corinthians 2:6-11). We elevate them to the level of being a human being rather than reduce them to the level of their behavior. Forgiveness is also surrendering the right to retaliation (see 1 Peter 3:8-9). Our lust for revengeful satisfaction drives our desire to see our enemy suffer. Forgiveness is an embracing of the responsibility of rehabilitation.

There is a difference between retaliation and recuperation. Retaliation seeks to penalize and punish (see Hebrews 10:28-31). Recuperation (discipline) seeks to rehabilitate and restore (see Hebrews 12:11). Those who sin must acknowledge their sin and willingly enter a recuperation process. When we confess, rehabilitation should become the order of the day. Further rebuke is needed only when there is a denial of culpability. Once confession is made, law is over. There is no longer a need for rebuke. No wonder the Holy Spirit says when we confess, God forgives. Above all, remember that each of us is perpetually in recovery and in need of rehabilitation because we will never avoid all sin.

What happens when your children fail to heed your warning not to play on dangerous equipment? When they fall and hurt themselves, they will delay coming to you if they know that they will receive only a rebuke—law but no grace. This delay may just magnify the problem. When they know that they will receive law *and* grace (transportation to the hospital), they will more readily come.

> We should never allow critics within nor without to turn the church away from its mission.

Pseudo-critics of Sin

The devil prompts critics to say, "Don't say anything to me about no church. I know all of these hypocrites in the church. I know so and so who is addicted to drugs, so and so who beats her husband, and so and so who writes bad checks." We ought to look them squarely in the eye and remind these critics that the church is a hospital for sinners not a haven for saints. It is not a reservation for those who have it made but a refuge for those who are trying to do better.

When critics point out the lifestyle of those who have not fully matured, we often feel guilty and embarrassed about them. Too often we hope the fallen believer would just silently and quickly go away and stop embarrassing us (see Luke 7:36-50). That is a wrong attitude. We should never allow critics within nor without to turn the church away from its mission. Ideally, when critics point out the sin of church members, we should call the critics into account for their behavior. Notice how Jesus did it. When His accusers pointed out the behavior of His disciples, rather than allowing them to excuse themselves away from confrontation, He called them into account for their behavior (see Matthew 15:1-3, John 8:1-9). For example, when someone asks, "Why does Henry Brown still gamble?" you ought to ask, "Why do you still dishonor your parents?" Instead of discussing someone else's behavior, confront the critic about his behavior.

Believers should hate sin as God does. Someone said, "I am against sin. I will fight it as long as I have a fist, I will kick it as long as I have a foot, and I will bite it as long as I have a tooth. When I am old, fistless, footless, and toothless, I will gum it till I go home to glory."

Without consulting anyone, preachers must preach the principle of practical righteousness. Through our preaching, we must challenge believers to avoid sinful behaviors. Through our preaching we must also console believers when they do sin. Without consulting with anyone, preachers must preach the practice that supports saints when they do sin. Imagine the Sunday morning sermon consisting of strategies for how the church will support an unwed mother. Imagine the preacher preaching that practice without consulting with the elders. In many cases that might be his last sermon—but until we wrestle the preaching of the practice away from the hierarchy, the church will never be free to vibrantly follow the vision of God.

PART 2

FAMILY

Chapter 6

THE JESUS KIND OF FAMILY

WHERE IS A REAL NEHEMIAH WHEN YOU NEED him? Where is the Nehemiah who sees the mess our families are in and willingly declares the message that will lead us out of this mess? Where is the Nehemiah who boldly recommends a practice that walks us into the principle.

Many have written many chapters and books about the family. So why am I writing more chapters? I am doing so because in my estimation, there are very few books containing advanced and spiritually healthy concepts about family. In fact, many of them completely miss the spiritual mark. Some have even attempted to create a new spiritual center and are successfully pedaling their poisonous propaganda to a population that is devoid of God's divine truths for the family.

I promised you that in this book I would be like Nehemiah—one who not only sees the family mess we are in, but one who also provides a God-ordained way out of that family mess. I promised to speak the truth to you, and I will continue to do so. So now here I am.

Within scripture, God has painted a definitive family portrait. In this section of the book, I will try to paint the nuances of that portrait. If you discover that you disagree, do know that I intend no malice. Please interpret all positive statements about females as nothing more than positive statements about females and not negative statements about males. Also, interpret all positive statements about males as nothing more than positive statements about males and not negative statements about females.

I am blessed to have been raised in a home with my father who was a very strong nurturing man who loved my mother and us. My mother was also a strong nurturing woman who was in subjection to my father. The dedication pages in my books *Good and Angry* (dedicated to my mother) and *The Power of the Tongue* (dedicated to my father) bear witness to this fact.

> Society and even organized religion have crushed the concepts of Scripture into a culturally sensitive mold. Unfortunately, all of us are victimized.

In spite of this strong nurturing, I am and have been victimized by our culture more than I could have ever imagined. In the early 1980s while living in Jonesboro, Arkansas, I wrote a weekly newspaper article for *The Jonesboro Sun*. For Mother's Day, I wrote an article entitled "Magnificent Mothers." Just a few weeks later for Father's Day, I wrote an article entitled "Faltering Fathers." Why did I compliment mothers but criticize fathers? I had no first-hand knowledge of a negligent father. My father was not a faltering father at all. My home experiences did not warrant such a negative assessment of fathers. Neither did my outside exposures within the community where I grew up warrant such an imbalance. Then why is there such a disparity? Why did I automatically criticize fathers and compliment mothers?

Unfortunately, this has become the norm for most pulpits. Have you ever heard a rebuke of mothers on Mother's Day? Why is there such disparity? I, too, am victimized by my environmental society. Our society has bought and paid for the myth that mothers are basically good; therefore they are always worthy of praise. The other side of this myth says that fathers are basically no good; therefore they are not worthy of any praise.

How did this happen? Society and even organized religion have crushed the concepts of Scripture into a culturally sensitive mold. Unfortunately, all of us are victimized. As a result there are some things that must be said, and I believe that God has preserved me for "such a time as this" to say them.

God has preserved me to remind all that the Jesus factor influences the family. Indeed the Jesus factor can make a healthy improvement in the quality of our family fellowship. Much too often however, we communicate with Jesus *only* when there is a crisis in our lives. This kind of communication style is preoccupied with getting the Lord to help us with our plans, rather than hearing His exciting plans for us. This kind of communication style limits our relationship with Him.

 These hard sayings of Jesus offer the very secrets of how to put Him first in our lives and begin to realize our full potential.

Jesus wants to show us a life that is far greater than any we have ever imagined. Often though, He must first speak hard words to wake us up. He positions these difficult sayings throughout Scripture, many of which we often skip over in search of teachings that appeal to us. Jesus presents soul-sized challenges with His offer to help us accomplish them. He may even confront us with a challenge that requires far greater power from Him than we have ever known. He seeks to show us greater victories than we have ever imagined.

Jesus has uttered some very hard sayings. Some are hard to interpret and others are hard to incorporate into life. Often, we prefer to believe that we can omit His hard sayings, as if those sayings provide no benefits at all. Yet, these hard sayings of Jesus offer the very secrets of how to put Him first in our lives and begin to realize our full potential. These sayings are bound within the training manual for a real Jesus-empowered religion.

Jesus multiplied five loaves of barley bread and a few pieces of fish and fed 5,000 people. However, He wanted to satisfy the deeper hunger and thirst that was in their heart. He claimed that He was "the bread of life" who came down from Heaven and could eternally satisfy their hunger and thirst (John 6:35).

In Jesus' day when people had worked to the point of exhaustion, they often said, "I have eaten my body and drunk my blood." In other words, they had given themselves completely to their task. When a leader called for the unreserved commitment of his followers, he demanded that they "eat his flesh and drink his blood." That was a colorful metaphor indicating total loyalty and allegiance. When Jesus uttered this hard saying about eating His flesh and drinking His blood, "the real Jesus" was inviting His disciples to a communion and a commitment with Him (see John 6:53-56).

Those who first heard His saying strongly objected, not because they misunderstood but because they understood all too well what He meant. They knew He was calling on them to accept Him as the son of God and to commit to constantly communing with Him. For their commitment, He promised to satisfy all their spiritual hungers and thirsts. Would not everyone readily participate in this kind of relationship? Surprisingly enough, those who first heard Jesus rejected His invitation. They refused to comply with the requirements of this kind of relationship. How willing are you to do differently? What great improvement will take place within your family fellowship if you did?

Chapter 7

THE SEARCH FOR SIGNIFICANCE

I AM PARTICULARLY GRATEFUL TO THOSE WHO HAVE shared with me their personal experiences. Feeling the hurt of those who have been trampled by the very ones whom God sent to console them continually agonizes my spirit. It is that feeling which was like a "fire shut up in my bones," that would not allow me to hold my peace and compelled me to pen these words about your search for significance. The selfish search for a pseudo-significance has torn too many families asunder.

What exactly did you say the last time you introduced yourself and began to talk to someone you didn't know? Why do we introduce ourselves by associating with someone or something that is perceived to be important? Could it be that we are searching for significance?

Their normal and natural needs drove Adam and Eve to search for significance. Unfortunately they searched away from their God-centered identity. Subsequently, they failed to find an adequate source for their significance. God created us with a normal and natural need for significance. Those normal and natural needs drive us to search for significance. Where we begin our search determines where we will end our search. Too often, we search for significance away from a God-centered identity. Where we begin determines where we will end. When we begin our search on the basis of a God-centered identity, we will do well, but when we begin our search off basis from a God-centered identity, we will end up not doing well.

When we search for significance away from our God-centered identity, we under-value what God gives us. He charged Adam to subdue and rule the fish, birds, and every living thing (see Genesis 1:26-28). How would Adam rule the birds of the air? Adam did not have a jet, helicopter, or even a hot-air balloon, yet he was to rule the birds of the air.

What God spoke happened. God ruled the universe through His spoken words. Adam would rule the birds of the air through his God-likeness. God had created them in

His image. His image consisted of the power to speak good words and perform good works. Adam would rule the birds through his spoken words. Adam could simply speak to the birds and they would obey. Imagine Adam walking through the forest and speaking to the bald eagle and the eagle would obey. Imagine walking beside the sea shore and speaking to the great white whale and the whale would obey. Yes, by created design Adam was the most significant of God's creation, but when Adam searched for significance off basis, outside a God-centered identity, Satan led him to under-value what God had given him.

Having a God-centered identity affects every member of a family.

In addition to the ruling significance that God had given Adam, God gave Adam and Eve spiritual status: They were blessed and positioned for prosperity (see Genesis 1:28). He also gave them social stimulus: fruitfulness and multiplica-tion (see Genesis 1:28), nutritious nurture, seeds for food (see Genesis 1:29, 2:9), and aesthetic beauty, "pleasing to the sight" (Genesis 2:9).

When we search for significance away from the basis of our God-centered identity, we over-value what Satan tells us. What Satan tells us leads to disbelief, doubt, and disobedience. Satan made Adam and Eve feel insignifi-cant by leading them to believe that God had withheld significance from them. God said, "If you eat, your circumstances will become worse," but Satan said, "If you eat, your circumstances will become better" (see Genesis 3:4-5 paraphrased). They ate in an attempt to be like a "god," when they were already like the one and only true God who had created them in His image.

What does this have to do with families? Having a God-centered identity affects every member of a family. A God-centered identity leads fathers to feel significant when they bring their children up in the discipline and instruction of the Lord. "Fathers, do not provoke your children to anger, but bring them up in the discipline and instruction of the Lord" (Ephesians 6:4). To bring them up is to train them. Training includes both a verbal explanation and a visible demonstration that entices correct behavior. Fathers who search for significance on the basis of their God-centered identity feel as significant as they want to feel when they bring their children up in the discipline and instruction of the Lord. Therefore, these fathers will never neglect their children or engage in any other off-centered experience to make themselves feel significant. As reinforcement we must applaud fathers who discipline and instruct their children in the Lord.

A God-centered identity leads children to feel significant when they obey and honor their parents, "Children, obey your parents in the Lord, for this is right. Honor your father and mother (which is the first commandment with a promise), so that it may be well with you, and that you may live long on the earth" (Ephesians 6:1-3). To honor means to assign the proper value and respond accordingly to that value. Children who search for significance on the basis of their God-centered identity feel as significant as they want to feel when they obey and honor their parents. Therefore, these children will never disobey nor neglect their parents in an effort to feel significant. As reinforcement we must applaud children who obey and honor their parents.

A God-centered identity leads a husband to feel significant when he loves his wife. "Husbands, love your wives, just as Christ also loved the church and gave Himself up for her… so husbands ought also to love their own wives as their own bodies. He who loves his own wife loves himself" (Ephesians 5:25, 28). Love is an attitude and an action caused by a need but regulated by relationship and resources. Husbands who search for significance on the basis of their God-centered identity feel as significant as they want to feel when they love their wives. Therefore, these husbands will never neglect their wives to do anything else or engage in any other experience to make them feel significant. How long has it been since you heard a husband bragging about how he loves his wife? As reinforcement we must applaud husbands who love their wives.

A God-centered identity leads a wife to feel significant when she submits to her husband. "Wives, be subject to your own husbands, as to the Lord…But as the church is subject to Christ, so also the wives ought to be to their husbands in everything" (Ephesians 5:22, 24). To submit is to arrange in an orderly fashion under the guidance of another. Wives who search for significance on the basis of their God-centered identity feel as significant as they want to feel when they submit themselves to their husbands. Therefore, these wives will never neglect being in submission to their husbands in order to do anything else or to engage in any other experience to make them feel significant. How long has it been since you heard a wife bragging about how she is in subjection to her husband? As reinforcement we must applaud wives who submit themselves to their husbands.

Significance on the basis of our God-centered identity provides peace and produces joy. Significance becomes a faith issue. We should walk by faith (what we hear from God), not sight (what people show us). God gives us our righteousness. Satan tells us we can achieve our righteousness off basis from a God-centered identity (see Luke 18:9-14). We must begin to speak more favorably about what we hear from God rather than about what we see, or even think we see.

Fathers, do you feel adequately significant when you are training your children? Children, do you feel adequately significant when you obey and honor your parents? Husbands, do you feel adequately significant when you love your wife? Wives, do you feel adequately significant when you are in subjection to your husband?

POWER-OVER VERSUS POWER-UNDER

Our significance regulates our influence. The two disciples of Jesus, James and John, desired to be significant. That desire formulated their divisive request. "They said to Him, 'Grant that we may sit, one on Your right and one on Your left, in Your glory'" (Mark 10:37). This divisive request resulted in an outburst of raw human emotions within the other disciples. "Hearing this, the ten began to feel indignant with James and John" (Mark 10:41).

God wants us to be significant. Contrasting the kingdom of the Gentiles with the kingdom of God, Jesus taught His disciples how to be significant. Jesus did not rebuke them for desiring to be significant. Rather, He taught them how to be significant. You are to be significant with God's approval. Never seek to reduce your significance. You are not behaving humbly when you say, "I am a nobody. I'm so stupid. I'm so slow. I'm a mess." You are behaving in an ungodly manner.

Do not seek to be significant as those of this world. They seek to be significant through power-over tactics. Those who exercise power-over tactics seek to lord over and exercise authority over others. "Calling them to Himself, Jesus said to them, 'You know that those who are recognized as rulers of the Gentiles lord it over them; and their great men exercise authority over them'" (Mark 10:42).

With power-over, you serve me. While you serve me, you are insignificant. Since you are insignificant, you become less influential. Power-over is the nature of the kingdom of this world. This world is set up to operate through power-over tactics. Your employer uses power-over skills. Someone is over you and he or she exercises authority over you. Imagine a policeman asking the suspect if he would *like* to "spread 'em."

Do seek to be significant as those of the kingdom of God. They seek to be significant through power-under tactics. Power-under tactics seek to lead as a servant and serve as a slave. "But it is not this way among you, but whoever wishes to become great among you shall be your servant; and whoever wishes to be first among you shall be slave of all" (Mark 10:43-44).

In power-under, I serve you. You are significant. Because you are significant, you become more influential. Power-under is the nature of the kingdom of God. God wants us to be significant. According to Matthew's account of the previously mentioned experience, the mother of James and John spoke their request to Jesus (see Matthew 20:20). Therefore, this request was a family issue. We must apply this principle within the family dynamic.

 Imagine a family where each family member serves the other family members. Imagine a family wherein each family member is significant.

The Proverbs 31 wife served her husband; that is power-under. He was significant and influential. "Her husband is known in the gates, when he sits among the elders of the land" (Proverbs 31:23). The leaders sat at the gates, the entrance to the walled city. They served as judges to settle disputes among the people. Her husband was known among the leaders whom he served.

The Proverbs 31 husband served his wife; that is power-under. She was significant and influential. "Her children rise up and bless her; her husband also, and he praises her" (Proverbs 31:28). The husband had affirmed his wife so much that the children had caught hold of the notion. Read the full proverb for a greater appreciation for the power-under search for significance within the family.

When a husband (father) affirms the significance of his wife to their children, the mother's influence with the children remains greatest. When a wife (mother) affirms the significance of her husband to their children, the father's influence with the children remains greatest. Children more readily obey parents whom they perceive to be significant and influential.

Imagine a family where each family member serves the other family members. Imagine a family wherein each family member is significant. Imagine a family wherein each family member is influential. Occasionally, one family member needs to remind others to adhere to power-under rather than power-over. Likely all family conflict surfaces through the exercise of power-over tactics.

Some suffering simply comes with the territory. "For even the Son of Man did not come to be served, but to serve, and to give His life a ransom for many" (Mark 10:45). The cross comes before the crown and the tomb comes before the throne. Therefore, all are not presently ready to seek significance through power-under. Yet, the search for significance through power-over has the potential to tear the fabric of family unity. Power-over is a disruptive issue within the family. Power–under is the only cure for ailing families.

Chapter 8

PERFORMANCE-BASED SIGNIFICANCE

GOD TRANSFORMS THE SPIRITUALLY DEAD INTO His workmanship:

> *And you were dead in your trespasses and sins, in which you formerly walked according to the course of this world, according to the prince of the power of the air, of the spirit that is now working in the sons of disobedience. Among them we too all formerly lived in the lusts of our flesh, indulging the desires of the flesh and of the mind, and were by nature children of wrath, even as the rest. But God, being rich in mercy, because of His great*

love with which He loved us, even when we were dead in our transgressions, made us alive together with Christ (by grace you have been saved)...For we are His workmanship, created in Christ Jesus for good works, which God prepared beforehand so that we would walk in them (Ephesians 2:1-5, 10).

From the original word translated as *workmanship* we received our English word *poem*. A poem is a skillfully composed production. Within a poem, words and phrases are consciously crafted to generate a desired impact. God transformed the formerly devastated people into His poem. As God's poem, His people are His remanufactured product. Being God's poem, His people have been skillfully composed, consciously crafted, and manufactured with adorable significance. Unfortunately, many people fail to recognize their God-given significance.

God condemns our power-over basis for significance. He endorses our power-under basis for significance. Those who have chosen to feel insignificant attempt to perform their way into feeling significant. Those who have chosen to feel insignificant will claim that others have made them feel insignificant, but no one can make another feel a particular way. If I could make people feel a particular way, I would make everyone feel financially favorable toward me.

Who are those who attempt to perform their way into significance? The active performer is afflicted by his desire to become significant. The active performer may be competent but compulsive. The active performer may suffer from the perfectionist syndrome. Often, they are guilty of overkill, an over-abundance of effort.

Martha may have been afflicted with this syndrome (see Luke 10:38-42). While her sister, Mary, was listening to the words of Jesus, Martha was distracted by what was unnecessary. Do you feel that you have to perform at a certain level to receive family approval and acceptance? Do you feel rejected? Do you feel that your self-worth declines when a family member critiques your performance? Do you become irrationally defensive toward that family member? Do you withhold emotional nurture from family members who dare to critique your performance? Do you disengage emotional connectedness from them?

When we feel unaccepted, we are likely to attempt to perform in order to feel significant. This feeling is the foundation for gang membership. Individuals who feel insignificant will endure the initiation ritual in order to be received into the gang family. Within the gang, they believe they will be significant. Children who feel their family significance are less likely to become members of a gang family.

The passive performer is afflicted by his desire to become significant. The passive performer is one who waits until someone or something acts upon him. Though the passive performer is not assertive, he may be competent but pseudo-humble. The passive performer fears failure and his fear of failure lulls him into inactivity. The one-talent man may have been afflicted with this syndrome (see Matthew 25:14-25).

Out of fear, he went away and hid his money doing nothing to generate a return.

 Imagine parents requiring newborns to do something before they granted them significance.

Do you feel incapable of performing at the level that will obtain family approval and acceptance? Do you feel your self-worth has declined due to poor performance, although no one has told you that? Do you become physically drained and/or pained at the very thought of performing? Do you become emotionally stressed at that thought? Do you look for ways to excuse accepting challenging assignments? Do you refuse to accept them for fear of failure, even though you have always succeeded?

Performance-based significance says, "I perform so that I can *become* significant." Therefore, performance-based significance relies on steroids to produce statistics (see Luke 18:9-14). Poem-based significance says, "I perform because I *am* significant." Therefore, poem-based significance reflects the process, not just the product. You will never find adequate significance in your accomplishments. Only within the grace of God will you discover lasting significance.

Imagine parents requiring newborns to do something before they granted them significance. Rather parents consider their children significant because the children *are,* not because the children *do.* The older we become, the more we rely on performance. Likely, you felt better liked as a babe when your significance came from being, not doing. If our performance determines our significance, the older we become the less significant we become, because whatever we are able to do now, likely we were able to do it better during our youth.

MYTHS

Some suffer from the myth that says, "Those who fail lose significance." When we subscribe to this erroneous thinking, we then believe that those who fail are unworthy of loving acceptance. This false belief causes us to emotionally victimize ourselves. Self-condemnation runs rampant. We feel that when we fail we are unworthy of love and deserve only to be punished. Deep-seated emotional issues surface. Some choose alcoholism as their escape route when they fail. They are unable to face reality sober. Your family's drunk may be suffering from this myth.

We feel bad because we feel bad about ourselves. And we punish ourselves because we feel bad about ourselves. We assign ourselves some punishment. We then fail to carry out the punishment. Then we feel even worse. For example, we say, "I am going to save $100 per week." For three weeks we keep our assignment, but the fourth week we go to the mall and spend $800. Now we feel bad. We punish ourselves. We decide to save $200 per week. This unrealistic goal keeps us in perpetual failure mode. Therefore, we can keep punishing ourselves.

This myth seems to have been the case with Judas:

> *Then when Judas, who had betrayed Him, saw that He had been condemned, he felt remorse and returned the thirty pieces of silver to the chief priests and elders and he threw the pieces of silver into the temple sanctuary and departed; and he went away and hanged himself (Matthew 27:3, 5).*

Judas saw that he had been condemned. How did he see that? Jesus never told him he was condemned. Jesus never treated him as if he were condemned. Jesus knew all along that Judas would betray Him. Yet, He treated Judas so well that the other disciples did not know it was Judas who would betray Jesus. Judas just conjured it up in his own mind that he was condemned. No doubt he believed that those who fail are worthy only of condemnation.

If Judas had gone to Him in repentance, Jesus would have forgivingly welcomed him. Why did Judas kill himself? He just believed that those who failed were worthy of death. A feeling of insignificance due to failure is a root cause of many suicides.

We need to affirm the truth of God about ourselves. We have sinned, but we are forgiven. We have sinned, but we are not unworthy of love. We have sinned, but we do not deserve punishment only.

Jesus is the propitiation, appeasement, and satisfaction—the adequate substitute—for sin (see 1 John 2:1-2, 4:10, Hebrews 10:16-19). He is the atoning sacrifice that has already satisfied God's justice demand for sin. Therefore, to trust in human goodness alone is to deny the atoning sacrifice of Jesus for sin. Unfortunately, many continue to believe that those who fail are unworthy of loving acceptance.

Michael Vick pled guilty, was sentenced, and served time in prison. When he was released from prison, many believed he should not be allowed to resume his NFL career. Though the dog fighting may have been extremely gross, should he not be allowed to recover from his past failure? Those who love animals exact a great amount of hatred toward this human being.

After being warned by God, Cain plotted and planned a grievous deed against his brother Abel. In spite of the premeditated nature of Abel's sin, God showed great mercy in protecting Cain from capital punishment by those who would retaliate against him (see Genesis 4:15).

How should the church respond if a church elder sins? Really, how should the church respond if a church elder becomes guilty of idolatry, thievery, or covetousness? Should the church commit itself to his continual recovery or to his constant rebuke?

How does the church usually respond? All too frequently, many believers desire that he be removed from office never ever again to serve in that capacity. A few others might take a stand-off position to see if the fallen one will rise again on his own. If he rises, he will then be received. If he fails to rise, the "church" will say justice has been served. How sad. The family of our biological procreation must ignore such nonsense, retrieve each fallen member, and restore him or her back to full family station and status. The church, our family by spiritual recreation, must ignore such nonsense, retrieve each fallen member, and restore him or her back to full church station and status. Not only must we preach that principle, we must preach a practice that implements that principle.

 We have been conditioned to believe that people should get what they deserve. The higher the position from which one falls, the better we feel about ourselves.

Do you feel emotionally inadequate when you are in the presence of the "good" family members? Have you emotionally disconnected from those "good" family members? God wants all to experience His forgiveness.

This false belief causes us to emotionally victimize others because of our own self-righteousness (see Luke 18:9-14). We feel that when others fail they are unworthy of love and deserve only to be punished (see Jonah 3:10-4:3). Violent attitudes erupt into violent behavior. We feel good about ourselves when others feel bad about themselves. We seek to punish others that we might feel better about ourselves.

Therefore, we seek to exonerate ourselves by making sure that the ones who fail are identified and punished.

We have been conditioned to believe that people should get what they deserve. The higher the position from which one falls, the better we feel about ourselves. Certain careers are always mentioned in the report of those who fail. When the preacher's or the policeman's son get into trouble, the news always mention his father's career. When the parent is the janitor or the bus driver, nothing is said about father's career. Why?

Unfortunately, many continue to believe that those who fail are unworthy of loving acceptance. Do you feel emotionally more adequate when you are contrasted with "bad" family members? Do you feel emotionally relieved when you disconnect from these family members? God wants all to experience His forgiveness. Nurture others as they experience the forgiveness of God (see Hebrews 4:14-16).

Pierced Together By Love!

The Bible references slavery numerous times. Many became slaves through economic misfortune while others became slaves through military conquest (see 2 Kings 5:2). It then should not surprise you to learn that God opposes both poverty and war, both of which lead to slavery.

The wise man Solomon declared, "The rich rules over the poor, and the borrower becomes the lender's slave" (Proverbs 22:7). Slavery was a socio-economic relationship wherein the slave held the minority of economic significance and social influence. The slave master held the majority of the economic significance and social influence. The slave master was the majority-dominating partner, while the slave was the minority-dominating partner. Therefore, those who borrow place themselves within a socio-economic servitude relationship. Now you know why God wants His people to be wealthy. "For the Lord your God will bless you as He has promised you, and you will lend to many nations, but you will not borrow; and you will rule over many nations, but they will not rule over you" (Deuteronomy 15:6).

Within the New Testament, God provided three extended submission sections of scripture: Ephesians 5:21-6:9, Colossians 3:18-4:9, and 1 Peter 2:13-3:22. He addressed the socio-economic relationship of slavery (see Colossians 3:22-4:6). He addressed the slave and the slave master. Principles of scripture paved the way for the eventual laws eradicating slavery, but while doing so, principles of scripture governed the attitudinal behavior of the slave through power-under rather than power-over tactics.

Slavery existed during the days of Abraham; therefore it existed before the time of Moses (see Genesis 17:12; 27, Deuteronomy 24:7; 23:15). Through the law of Moses, God regulated slavery of Hebrews by other Hebrews:

> "If you buy a Hebrew slave, he shall serve for six years; but on the seventh he shall go out as a free man without payment. If he comes alone, he shall go out alone; if he is the husband of a wife, then his wife shall go out with

> *him. If his master gives him a wife, and she bears him*
> *sons or daughters, the wife and her children shall belong*
> *to her master, and he shall go out alone. But if the slave*
> *plainly says, 'I love my master, my wife and my children;*
> *I will not go out as a free man,' then his master shall*
> *bring him to God, then he shall bring him to the door or*
> *the doorpost. And his master shall pierce his ear with*
> *an awl; and he shall serve him permanently" (Exodus*
> *21:2-6).*

The law restricted the length of slavery to six years (see verse 2a). During those six years a man could marry, father children, and live with his family (see verse 4a). After he had served for six years, he was free to leave his slave master, wife, and children or he could remain with them (see verses 4-5).

A father who chose to remain received a pierced ear (see verses 5-6). We must thank God for fathers who willingly pierce their ear. A pierced ear indicated that a father loved his master, wife, and children more than he loved his personal freedom. Therefore, he chose to remain with them permanently. He recognized that his relationship with them was more valuable than his personal freedom.

A pierced ear also indicated that a father loved his family more than he loved his *personal finances:*

> *"If your kinsman, a Hebrew man or woman, is sold to you,*
> *then he shall serve you six years, but in the seventh year*
> *you shall set him free. When you set him free, you shall*
> *not send him away empty-handed. You shall furnish*
> *him liberally from your flock and from your threshing*

floor and from your wine vat; you shall give to him as the Lord your God has blessed you. You shall remember that you were a slave in the land of Egypt, and the Lord your God redeemed you; therefore I command you this today. It shall come about if he says to you, 'I will not go out from you,' because he loves you and your household, since he fares well with you; then you shall take an awl and pierce it through his ear into the door, and he shall be your servant forever. Also you shall do likewise to your maidservant. It shall not seem hard to you when you set him free, for he has given you six years with double the service of a hired man; so the Lord your God will bless you in whatever you do" (Deuteronomy 15:12-18).

A pierced ear visibly indicated a father's affectionate allegiance toward his family. He loved his master, wife, and children more than he loved his personal finances; therefore, he would give up economic resources to remain with them (see verse 16). He realized that his relationship with them was more valuable than his personal finances. We must thank God for fathers who willingly pierce their ear.

Unfortunately, we have sacrificed family on the altar of personal freedom and finances. If you abandon your wife and children for personal freedom and finances, you will shortly exchange it for another man's enslavements and expenses (ex-wife and children). Young men think that personal freedom and finances will be permanent, but older men know that it is only temporary. God wants you to implement a visible indicator of your affectionate allegiance toward your family.

Chapter 9

THE GOD FACTOR INFLUENCES THE FAMILY

HROUGH ADAM, GOD CREATED THE HUMAN RACE.
Through Abraham, He created the Hebrew race. God
continued the creation of the Hebrew race through
Abraham's son, Isaac, then through Isaac's son, Jacob, and
then through Jacob's son, Judah.

God created the Hebrew race to be blessed themselves and
to become a blessing to others. To be blessed was to be positioned for prosperity. To be positioned for prosperity was to
be favorably synchronized with people and circumstances.

Jacob's son Joseph personified Jesus because he was a type of Christ. Like Jesus, Joseph was the favored son of his father (see Genesis 37:1-11). Unfortunately, the favor of his father evoked a raging jealousy from his brothers, so they sold him (see Genesis 37:12-35).

Within each biblical narrative, we must ask, "Where is God and what is He doing?" Where is God and what is He doing within this Joseph narrative? Even in captivity, Joseph faithfully served both his earthy master and his heavenly master (see Genesis 39:1-9). The Joseph story was not just about Joseph being a good model for us but about what God is doing. Even though the story does tell precisely of Joseph's behavior, a broader perspective still exists. Through His providential care, God's sovereignty successfully guided Joseph. This historical fact convinces us to believe this contemporary fact: The guiding hand of God is with us.

What does His guiding hand enable us to do? His guiding hand enables us to say, "You sold me but God sent me" (see Genesis 45:4-8). Joseph's problem was compounded by his dream of his brothers bowing down to him (see Genesis 37:5-11). Although his brothers sold him intending for him to be in slavery, God was sending him that He might bring about the salvation of an entire nation.

His guiding hand enables us to say, "You meant evil against me, but God meant it for good" (Genesis 50:20). Joseph's problem was concluded by his vision of his brothers bowing down to him (see Genesis 42:6-7). Although his brothers intended evil to come upon Joseph, God put evil on hold and brought about much good. God even brought about good on behalf of Joseph's brothers, the ones who initiated the evil against him.

 Discipleship never immunizes us from conspiracies.

The guiding hand of God is with you. Then, God was with Joseph every step of the way. Now, God is with you every step of the way (see Genesis 28:10-22). God wants you to courageously confront adversity peacefully (see Hebrews 12:5-6). Joseph's firm faith in this fact enabled the favorable conclusion of the story as you will later observe.

What would you think if you discovered that your brothers and sisters had conspired against you? How would you feel? How would you respond? Joseph's brothers developed a passionate hatred for him (see Genesis 37:3-5). Their revengeful hatred drove them to conspire against Joseph (see verses 12-20). Yes, they plotted and planned a devious scheme to destroy their brother Joseph.

Discipleship never immunizes us from conspiracies. We can, however, withstand a revengefully conspired family vendetta. How? Let us consider proven mechanisms that will help us to withstand even a wicked family vendetta.

1. **Soak your face.** Joseph soaked his face; he just cried (see Genesis 50:17). He had cried before (see Genesis 42:24, 43:30, 45:1-2, 14-15). We,

too, may need to soak our face in tears of release. Open the healthy valves of our emotional release. Maintain our emotional health.

2. **Stay in your place.** Joseph stayed in his place (see Genesis 50:19). To stay in his place meant he was staying out of God's place (see verse 20). We, too, must stay in our place. Close the desire for unhealthy retaliation. Maintain our intellectual health.

3. **Save your grace.** Joseph saved his grace. He had enjoyed God's acceptance and approval in the past (see Genesis 50:20). Indeed, he planned to keep on enjoying the blessings of God (see verse 21). We, too, must save our grace. Keep the favor of God abounding. Maintain our spiritual health. Satan becomes angry when believers receive favor from God. He will express his displeasure and cause conspiracies against you, your family, your congregation, and/or its teacher. You can withstand even a revengefully conspired family vendetta.

THE FAMILY FACTOR INFLUENCES THE FAMILY

Family has a responsibility to family. We are individuals, but we are not to be isolated from one another. We are not here to do our own thing, in spite of, and disregarding others. Family has a responsibility for and to family members.

Husbands and wives have a responsibility to each other. Parents and children have a responsibility to each other. Family responsibility, however, extends beyond father, mother, and children. God's original design extends beyond just the parents and the children. It involves more than just a responsibility of the parents to the children and the children to the parents. Even when the parents have fulfilled their responsibility to the children, and children have fulfilled their responsibility to the parents, responsibility does not end there. Which other members share a responsibility to each other? Who are the family members who share a responsibility to one another? Uncles and aunts share a responsibility to the family. They share responsibility to the nieces and nephews in the family. Nieces and nephews share responsibility to uncles and aunts in the family. They share a responsibility to pursue a meaningful relationship with each other.

Abram, whose name was later changed to Abraham, is the central character in Genesis chapter 13. Abram had a relationship with his nephew, Lot. Abram carried his nephew with him:

> *Now Lot, who went with Abram, also had flocks and herds and tents. And the land could not sustain them while dwelling together, for their possessions were so great that they were not able to remain together. And there was strife between the herdsmen of Abram's livestock and the herdsmen of Lot's livestock. Now the*

Canaanite and the Perizzite were dwelling then in the land (Genesis 13:5-7).

Notice the next verse very carefully: "So Abram said to Lot, 'Please let there be no strife between you and me, nor between my herdsmen and your herdsmen, for we are brothers'" (verse 8). Abraham pursued a meaningful and peaceful relationship with his nephew. "Is not the whole land before you? Please separate from me; if to the left, then I will go to the right; or if to the right, then I will go to the left" (verse 9).

When the conflict surfaced, Abram the uncle offered a solution to minimize the conflict with Lot, his nephew. When there are issues that threaten the peace, it requires someone to be mature enough to offer a solution. Now listen to what Abraham said: "If to the left, then I will go to the right; or if to the right, then I will go to the left" (verse 9). What happened next is very interesting:

Lot lifted up his eyes and saw all the valley of the Jordan, that it was well watered everywhere—this was before the Lord destroyed Sodom and Gomorrah—like the garden of the Lord, like the land of Egypt as you go to Zoar. So Lot chose for himself all the valley of the Jordan, and Lot journeyed eastward. Thus they separated from each other (verses 10-11).

Lot chose. The point I want to emphasize is that Abraham considered peace to be more valuable than sustenance. He said whichever way Lot chose to go, he would go the opposite. Our peaceful relationship is more valuable than the things we own. Abraham valued peace so much that he was willing to suffer a temporary loss of sustenance. Why? Because he felt a responsibility to the family. Family responsibility extends not only to brothers and sisters. It extends even to uncles and aunts, and nieces and nephews, and even beyond.

Brothers and sisters share a responsibility to their brothers and sisters. Brothers and sisters on many occasions must stand up and bargain for the lifeblood of their brothers and sisters. Notice what happened in the story about Joseph and his brothers:

> *When they saw him from a distance and before he came close to them, they plotted against him to put him to death. They said to one another, "Here comes this dreamer! Now then, come and let us kill him and throw him into one of the pits; and we will say, 'A wild beast devoured him.' Then let us see what will become of his dreams!" But Reuben heard this and rescued him out f their hands and said, "Let us not take his life." Reuben further said to them, "Shed no blood. Throw him into this pit that is in the wilderness, but do not lay hands on him"—that he might rescue him out of their hands, to restore him to his father (Genesis 37:18-22).*

One brother assumes responsibility for the life of another brother. One brother was against ten, but brothers and sisters on many occasions must stand up when one sibling is suffering injustice at the hands of another. They must stand up and say, "That's not right!" Reuben bargained for the lesser of two evils. He did not want to take his brother's life (verses 21-22).

Abuse your brothers and sisters if you will; it may very likely come back to you years later. Years later, Joseph was in charge of the sustenance in Egypt. His brothers were hungry and without food. They were at his mercy. They were in the presence of their brother, Joseph, but did not recognize him. I don't know how many years it had been, but likely their conscience had bothered them all the while. "Then they said to one another, 'Truly we are guilty concerning our brother, because we saw the distress of his soul when he pleaded with us, yet we would not listen; therefore, this distress has come upon us'" (Genesis 42:21).

 What does your family relationship say about your Christianity?

Apparently when they decided to throw Joseph into the pit, he begged for his life. They could remember the anguish on his face. Reuben answered them, saying, "Did I not tell you, 'Do not sin against the boy'; and you would not listen? Now comes the reckoning for his blood'" (Genesis 42:22). In essence, Rueben said, "I told you when you planned to do that, that you should not do it."

Family responsibility extends to brothers and sisters. We should responsibly stand up and bargain for the support of brothers and sisters. What kind of relationship do you have with your brothers and sisters? Are you angry with your brothers and sisters because you think your parents had favorites? Why are you angry with your sister? She's not the one who showed the favoritism. Are you angry at your brother because he had a chance to drive the car? If you would have done what your father had told you to do, he would have let you drive the car as well.

What does your family relationship say about your Christianity? You come to worship and call people, whom you have known less than six months, "brother" and "sister," but at the same time you refuse to communicate with your blood brother and sister who grew up in the same house as you, ate from the same plate, and probably wore the same undergarments at times. Even when brothers and sisters have mistreated you, forgive them. Family relationships are too important to neglect.

Family responsibility extends even to in-laws. Fathers-in-law, mothers-in-law, sons-in-law, daughters-in-law, brothers-in-law, and sisters-in-law share a responsibility to the family. This in-law relationship existed between Moses and his father-in-law. In Exodus chapter 18, Moses' father-in-law gave him advice (see verses 17-23). He gave him a strategy. He recommended appointing people to help and then dividing their responsibilities: Some of these appointed leaders would be over 1,000 people, some over 100, some over fifty, and some over ten. Moses' father-in-law recommended they bring the most devastating issues to Moses so that he could decide.

In-laws share a responsibility to accept profitable advice from their in-laws. Moses could have stood up and said,

"Listen, man, let me tell you something. You raised your daughter, but you're not raising me." Instead he listened to his father-in-law because his father-in-law was trying to help him—and it relieved a tremendous burden from his shoulders.

In-laws have a responsibility to share and relate to the family. They should not assume that whatever is being said to them is because someone is trying to get in their business or run their house. Some in-laws are genuinely concerned about your well-being. What kind of relationship do you have with your in-laws? Sometime in-laws have become out-laws. Isn't it interesting that in-laws don't want your advice, but they have no problems asking for your money? Daddy-in-law can give you his money but not his advice. Perhaps if you had taken his advice, you wouldn't need his money.

Can you imagine Moses rejecting the influence of his father-in-law? Would you accept advice from your in-laws? What kind of relationship do you have with your mother-in-law? Are you glad when your mother-in-law comes to visit? Or do you say, "She can't take care of her own house, so how can she help me?" Listen to the advice and determine its quality.

Grandparents share a responsibility to the family. What is the grandparents' responsibility? Grandparents should participate in the responsibility of teaching and training their grandchildren. This is a biblical concept:

> *"Now, O Israel, listen to the statutes and the judgments which I am teaching you to perform, so that you may*

live and go in and take possession of the land which the Lord, the God of your fathers, is giving you...Only give heed to yourself and keep your soul diligently, so that you do not forget the things which your eyes have seen and they do not depart from your heart all the days of your life; but make them known to your sons and your grandsons" (Deuteronomy 4:1, 9).

He said to teach your sons and your sons' sons. Sounds like grandchildren to me. All are to teach their children, but there is also a responsibility to teach the grandchildren. Now why in the world would the Lord assign such a responsibility as that? In most families grandparents are older. In most families, grandparents are more stable economically and intellectually. Often they are more stable spiritually. In many instances, they have a wealth of abundance to share.

Ensure that your children spend time with their grandparents. They're not there to aggravate them, but there to hang around so that they might absorb and benefit. I'm not talking about sending them to their grandparents because you want to go to the movies and you need a baby sitter. Arrange for them to spend quality time with their grandparents.

The responsibility extends beyond mother and father. When we fulfill our family responsibility, we then live the best quality of life. Grandparents are the solution for the family. The government is not going to salvage the family. The family must salvage itself. The time is past when grandparents can say, "I have raised mine and I'm through with it."

The Suspicion Factor Influences the Family

In the temporary absence of their father, Joseph's brothers mistreated him (see Genesis 37:12-20), so now in the permanent absence of their father, they assumed that Joseph would mistreat them (see Genesis 50:15). Because of their own guilty conscience, they suspected that Joseph would seek revenge.

A suspicion is an unsubstantiated belief. That unsubstantiated belief may be true or it may be false. False suspicions create the same feelings and solicit the same responses as if they were true. With unsubstantiated ammunition, you treat the person as if they've done what you suspect.

One day Adam told Eve that he was going out and would return soon. However, he did not return until late and Eve was really angry. "What have you been doing all day?" she asked. "I'm sure you are hiding something from me. Did you meet anyone?"

Adam said, "You know quite well there is no one else alive." He then shrugged his shoulders and went to sleep. As soon as he was asleep, Eve, still full of suspicion, began to count his ribs.

Suspicions will deteriorate our healthy fellowship. Suspicion will deceive our vision. Suspicion will cause us to see what is not even in existence. Because of their suspicion, Joseph's brothers saw a grudge within him when no grudge was within him (see Genesis 50:15). Because of their suspicion, Joseph's brothers saw revenge within him when no revenge was within him. Why did Joseph's brothers see a grudge and revenge within Joseph? Suspicion caused them to see what was absent. Their own guilty conscience deceived their vision.

Suspicion will destroy our vision. Suspicion will cause us to fail to see what is in existence. Because of their suspicion, Joseph's brothers failed to see the forgiveness that was within him even though he stated it to them (see Genesis 45:4-11). Because of their suspicion, Joseph's brothers failed to see the forgiveness that was within him even though he showed it to them for five years (see Genesis 45:11–Genesis 49:33). Why did Joseph's brothers fail to see the forgiveness that was within Joseph? Suspicion caused them to fail to see what was present. Their own guilty conscience destroyed their vision.

 It will do no good simply to talk about strong family relationships or preach about it.

Suspicion will cause us to make false statements about and to others. Earlier, they lied to their father about Joseph, causing him to believe that a wild animal had killed Joseph (see Genesis 37:31-35). Later, they lied to Joseph about their father (see Genesis 50:15-17).

Suspicion will cause us to lie to and about ourselves. Earlier, they had lied to their father about themselves (see Genesis 37:32). Later, they lied to Joseph about themselves (see Genesis 50:17). They were servants of Satan not God (see John 8:44). Their own guilty conscience afflicted what they saw and said. Suspicion will deteriorate your fellowship (see Titus 1:15-16).

God wants you to break free from all suspicion. Formulate a conclusion only after you sufficiently deliberate upon validating evidences. Repent of allowing suspicion to deceive and/or destroy your vision. Resolve never again to allow suspicion to deceive and/or destroy your vision.

In volume one of this book series, we studied the necessity of implementing a practice that will honor the principle. It will do no good simply to talk about strong family relationships or preach about it. God wants each family to affectionately bond together. How can we bond? We must implement a practice that will honor the principle; otherwise nothing changes. Therefore, I recommend a simple but successful practice that will increase family intimacy.

Family Day

Select a day each month to be family day. Here are the parameters:

1. Tell other families what your family day is.

2. On that day, prepare a full-course family meal.

3. Each family member is to participate simultaneously in the preparation of that full-course family meal.

4. Each member is to participate in the preparing, cooking, eating, and cleaning up.

5. All members must share fairly in the work.

6. Every family member must be in the kitchen throughout the entire period of time.

7. During the entire preparation, eating, and cleaning up, there is to be no television, telephone, stereo, iPod, email, texting, or any other distractions.

8. Only verbal conversation among family members is allowed.

9. No one should be allowed to be excused.

10. Each month prepare a different meal.

After eating such a sumptuous meal, I know that you have relaxed, put your stones back into your bag, and have begun to feel guilty for having considered throwing them in the first place. Someone said that men are from Mars and women are from Venus. The truth is that men are not from Mars and women have no need to go to Venus. When Dr. Harold Redd said, "Man is from God and woman is from man," I believe he accurately articulated the apostle Paul's inspired understanding of the matter at hand (see 1 Corinthians 11:3, 8).

The God-given paradigm is best. Even when there seem to be outcomes that beg to differ, God's paradigm for the family is best. So, young man, marry her before you father children by her (see 1 Timothy 5:14). Husband, love her and serve acceptably as the head of your wife. Wife, serve acceptably, being in submission to your husband. Father, educate your children all the way to maturity. Child, honor and obey your parents (see Ephesians 5:22-6:4). If you will unashamedly pledge your total loyalty and allegiance to God's family order, we can quickly climb out of the mess we are in. If not, go ahead and order extra Lysol, for the stench will begin soon.

PART 3

FINANCES

Chapter 10

ECONOMIC MAKEOVER: ACQUIRING ECONOMIC RESOURCES

THROUGH MY COUNSELING MINISTRY, I AM BROUGHT face to face with the economic woes of many families. Because so many give me so much access to information about their financial affairs, I have some insight of the personal financial landscape of our world. While I am grateful for this learning, I feel the pain of those who have been misguided. Often, the very people (parents) whom God gave to educate—that is, to provide visible demonstrations and verbal explanations of financial management—have failed to do so, thus harming rather than helping their children. Though I am not even on the same planet with financial experts, I do believe that the advice that I give here will point you in the right direction. Even though you may not become independently wealthy, someone should say something about God.

> Whenever someone violates God's system—whether an individual, company, city, county, or country—ill results follow.

Our culture needs a Nehemiah—one who not only sees the mess we are in but one who can apply God's solution to fix it. There are few areas as messy as our finances, both personal and corporate. The economic situation the world is in today is in large part due to the financial misdealing of a few people. Now, the rest of the world is suffering the consequences. We are not entirely innocent, however, and I will address that situation also in this section as I attempt to speak the truth about a situation that has thrived on mistruth and deception.

God designed the entirety of the universe as a system. Actually, the universe consists of systems within a system. Within the universe, He designed His economic system. He created patterns, principles, and procedures within His economic system. Patterns, principles, and procedures are established ways of doing things. God created them to guide in the acquiring and to guard in the dispersing of economic resources (see Genesis 1:26-31).

God seeks to manage His creation. He deputized Adam and Eve as custodial stewards of His creation. Throughout human history God has sought to govern the acquiring and dispersing of His economic resources. The Bible reveals God's economic system (see 1 Timothy 6:7-19). Trouble flares up when we violate God's system. Whenever someone violates God's system—whether an individual, company, city, county, or country—ill results follow.

God's economic system governs the acquiring of wealth. God gives us the power to make wealth (see Deuteronomy 8:18). Certainly, it is He who desires for us to receive and accumulate economic resources. As a matter of fact, riches are called blessings from the Lord (see Proverbs 10:22). Yes, God designed His economic system not to deprive us but to lavish upon us His economic resources.

God's economic system allows for the acquiring of wealth through commerce—the buying and selling of property (see James 4:13-15). Those who engage in business to make a profit do so according to the will of God.

SELLING YOUR INDUSTRIAL PROPERTY

God's economic system allows for the selling of one's industrial property—that is, property created through the production of your physical energy. When you sell the work of your hands, you are selling your industrial property (see Genesis 2:12, 3:19, Matthew 20:1-8, Ephesians 4:28).

God deposited the gold and the good of the land within human grasp. Therefore, He desired for Adam to work and accumulate those resources (see Genesis 2:12, 3:19). Jesus described the kingdom of Heaven as a landowner who purchased the industrial property (labor of their hands) from several workers (see Matthew 20:1-8).

God charged those who had been converted to engage in the selling of their industrial property. "He who steals must steal no longer; but rather he must labor, performing with his own hands what is good, so that he will have something to share with one who has need" (Ephesians 4:28). God recommends selling industrial property as a spiritual experience for those who have formerly been negligent.

When a beautician styles her customer's hair, she is selling her industrial property. When a welder mends a broken pipe, he is selling his industrial property. When a seamstress makes a dress for the bride, she is selling her industrial property. Workers on the assembly line at General Motors who attach the mirrors to the cars, or place the seats in position, or screw the wheels in place are selling industrial property. Through the physical energy that God gives, He provides economic resources.

Jesus used the buying and selling of industrial property to illustrate the kingdom of Heaven. No one can dispute the fact that buying and selling industrial property honors God's economic system. With God's divine approval, one may sell his or her industrial property in order to acquire economic resources. Although selling industrial property is an honorable means of generating income, it has its limitations. It requires the seller to be on location servicing the need. If the welder leaves work, he does not make any money while he is gone. The selling of industrial properties limits the revenue to what the seller is worth. The seller is paid only once for his industrial property. Normally, we receive only one day's pay for one day's labor. Therefore, each laborer must continually offer his or her labor in order to continually receive income. The selling of industrial property does not provide residual or recurring income.

SELLING YOUR INTELLECTUAL PROPERTY

God's economic system allows for the selling of our intellectual property—that is, property that results from the production of our mind. These can be logos, designs, paintings, and literary pieces such as books, music, and songs (see Genesis 1:26-28, 41:38-45, Daniel 2:46-49). God is the source of man's intellectual capacity. Therefore, He initially provided Adam with the intellectual capacity to rule the entire universe (see Genesis 1:26-28).

When Pharaoh dreamed a dream, initially no one could interpret it. Subsequently, Joseph interpreted his dream, and Pharaoh rewarded Joseph with position and power through which he received economic resources (see Genesis 41:14-49). Joseph sold his intellectual property. Through the intellectual capacity that God gave to Joseph, God provided economic resources making Joseph wealthy.

 God has given you great intellectual capacity. With it, you ought to create something of economic value.

King Nebuchadnezzar also dreamed a dream. Initially, no one could interpret his dream. Subsequently, Daniel interpreted his dream, and Nebuchadnezzar rewarded Daniel with position and power through which he received economic resources (see Daniel 2:46-49). Through the intellectual capacity that God gave to Daniel, God provided economic resources making Daniel wealthy.

When an artist produces a song, he is selling his intellectual property. When an author writes books, he is selling his intellectual property. When a person develops computer software, he is selling his intellectual property. Selling intellectual properties generates economic resources over and over again. The artist produced the song once, but he receives revenue (residual income or royalties) each time his songs are sold or played.

God has given you great intellectual capacity. With it, you ought to create something of economic value. There is no reason why you should not create at least one stream of income from selling your intellectual property. Many of you reading this book have neglected to utilize your intellectual capacity to generate economic resources for yourself. Some have dreamed and imagined, but have never moved forward.

SELLING YOUR INVESTMENT PROPERTY

God's economic system also allows for selling investment property—property that you accumulate. One may sell the accumulated property itself (see Acts 4:34-35, 37, Matthew 13:44-46, 19:16-21, 25:1-10). Or one may sell the usage of the accumulated property (see Matthew 21:33-34).

The sale of investment property gave the early church a boost of favoritism. New converts sold their property and possessions and distributed the proceeds to the apostles so that they might satisfy the financial need of others (see Acts 2:43-45). This benevolent expression gave the early church favor among those in Jerusalem, which resulted in numerous converts (see verse 47). The believers kept on selling their investment property. "For there was not a needy person among them, for all who were owners of land or houses would sell them and bring the proceeds of the sales and lay them at the apostles' feet, and they would be distributed to each as any had need" (Acts 4:34-35). Had members not had investment property, their impact would not have been felt within the community.

Those who sold their houses must have owned more than one house because if they sold the one house that they owned, then they themselves would be in need. The Bible says that they sold so that no one would have need. Obviously, the members owned more than one house as an investment. Investment property gave credibility to the early church.

Imagine the positive impact within a community if a congregation or the members of a congregation banded together to purchase its members' homes that were about to go into foreclosure. The purchase group could then rent the houses back to the members so that they and their families would not have to relocate. This joint venture could spare those who had suffered a misfortune much anguish and embarrassment. Their credit scores would also be preserved.

Certainly, some with impure motives would rush to become affiliated with that congregation. Many others, however, out of pure motives would highly value the compassionate posture of a congregation that enabled its members. In any case and in a relatively short time, everyone within hearing distance would know and most would speak favorably of the congregation's benevolent gestures.

The owner may sell the use of the accumulated property (see Matthew 21:33-34). In this instance, the ownership of the property remains with the initial owner, but someone just pays for the use of the property. With this transaction, the original owner receives payment time and time again throughout the course of the rental period.

Money is an accumulated property. Those who lend money are selling the use of accumulated property (see Matthew 25:14-27). Farmers (investors) deposit seed in the earth to receive a rate of return (see Matthew 13:3-8, Genesis 26:12-13). Investors deposit money in the bank to receive a rate of return.

Chapter 11

GIFTS

W E MAY ACQUIRE ECONOMIC RESOURCES through gifts. God is the master gift-giver. In the beginning, God gave economic gifts to Adam and Eve (see Genesis 1:29). Gifts are God's way of delivering economic resources to His people. Therefore, learn to receive gifts.

RELATIONSHIP GIFTS

Relationship gifts are given primarily because of relationship. Jesus spoke the parable of the man who planted a vineyard and rented it out to vine growers to teach His disciples about relationship gifts (see Luke 20:9-14). Although he rented his vineyard to vine growers, the owner of the vineyard did have a son. When the vineyard owner sent his slave to receive his rental revenue, the vine growers refused to honor his request. Again, the vineyard owner sent a second and a third slave, who was in turn also spurned. When the vineyard owner sent his son, the vine growers reasoned that the son would receive ownership of the vineyard because of his relationship to the owner. Therefore, they killed him.

This story illustrates how the people of God rejected God's prophets time and time again. Eventually, God sent His Son, Jesus. They killed Him. Nevertheless, in both instances the inheritance was to be passed on to the son because of relationship. Because of his relationship to his father, the prodigal son received his inheritance from his father (see Luke 15:11-12). Why did the son receive economic resources? He received them simply because of his relationship.

Our first economic resources came to us because of relationship. After we were born, our parents gave us food and clothing. Why? They gave to us because of relationship. Our parents did not give food and clothing to the neighbors' children. Imagine parents withholding necessities from newborns because they had no money to buy.

At times the recipient needs to receive the gift in order to feel whole, but at other times the giver needs to give the gifts in order to feel whole. Parents feel whole when they give gifts to their children. God feels whole when we receive gifts from Him.

All of life is not a reward, but if you are not receiving any reward gifts from God, you are probably being disobedient to His Word.

REWARD GIFTS

Reward gifts are given in response to approved behavior. They are gifts given as an honorarium for some deed done. God loves to give reward gifts. "But you shall remember the Lord your God, for it is He who is giving you power to make wealth, that He may confirm His covenant which He swore to your fathers, as it is this day" (Deuteronomy 8:18). God desires to show the world how He appreciates the good behavior of His people. His giving power to make wealth confirms His covenant. He proves Himself by His gifts to His people. Time and time again, the heathens heard about how well God had provided for His people.

Jesus talked about those who received gifts because they had first given (see Luke 6:38). He asked a rich ruler to give (see Luke 18:18-30). The rich ruler thought that Jesus was trying to take economic resources from him, but instead Jesus was trying to deliver gifts to the rich ruler. After His dialogue with His disciples, Jesus informed Peter that those who had given would be given a hundred times as much as they had given.

All of life is not a reward, but if you are not receiving any reward gifts from God, you are probably being disobedient to

His Word. If you are receiving no reward gifts from anyone else, you are probably living outside the favor range of your contemporaries.

RECUPERATION GIFTS

Recuperation gifts are given to those who have suffered a misfortune resulting in a deficit. Therefore, recuperation gifts are designed to restore adequacy or wholeness. Jesus told the rich ruler to give a recuperation gift to the poor: "When Jesus heard this, He said to him, 'One thing you still lack; sell all that you possess and distribute it to the poor, and you shall have treasure in heaven; and come, follow Me'" (Luke 18:22).

Zaccheus understood the value of giving recuperation gifts. He desired to give one-half of his possessions to the poor. "Zaccheus stopped and said to the Lord, 'Behold, Lord, half of my possessions I will give to the poor, and if I have defrauded anyone of anything, I will give back four times as much'" (Luke 19:8).

ECONOMIC MAKEOVER: DISBURSING ECONOMIC RESOURCES

God's economic system governs the disbursing of our wealth. God gives us the power to make wealth but He also desires to manage our use of that wealth.

Kingdom of God First, God guides us to disburse economic resources into the kingdom of God. In the 2008 presidential race, the winner, Barack Obama, raised a record $639 million. In the midst of a recession, Americans increased their political contributions while decreasing their church contributions. For change, people trust government more than they trust God. What a shame!

Tithes God guides His people to disburse economic resources into the kingdom of God through tithes. Tithing is a system specifically regulated by Heaven. It is done as a percentage (10 percent; see Hebrews 7:1-7, Leviticus 27:30-32), and as a priority (the first 10 percent; see Deuteronomy 26:1-10, Genesis 4:4). (For an in-depth discussion on tithes, read *Faith, Family, and Finances: Volume One.*)

> God authorizes gifts for seed. These are given as a means of planting seed within the kingdom of God.

Offerings. God guides His people in dispersing economic resources into the kingdom of God through offerings. The offering is a system categorically regulated by the heart (see Exodus 35:4, 21, 26, 29). (For an in-depth discussion on tithes, see *Faith, Family, and Finances: Volume One.*)

Gifts. God guides His people in dispensing economic resources into the kingdom of God through gifts. He authorizes recuperation gifts that are given for the need. "For Macedonia and Achaia have been pleased to make a contribution for the poor among the saints in Jerusalem" (Romans

15:26). Gifts are to be given into the kingdom of God when there is a need within the kingdom of God. The believers in Macedonia and Achaia gave gifts to the poor among the saints who were living in Jerusalem.

God authorizes gifts for seed. These are given as a means of planting seed within the kingdom of God. Gifts for seed are given into the kingdom of God in order to receive a return blessing from God. Yes, planting seed within the kingdom of God is an appropriate expression of faith toward God's past, present, and future expressions of grace. The apostle Paul desired the Philippians to give to him not because he needed something but so that they would receive a blessing (see Philippians 4:15-19). Ezra gave a financial gift into the kingdom of God in order to receive the protective favor of God for his journeys (see Ezra 8:21-31).

God guides His people to disperse economic resources into the kingdom of man. He authorizes us to pay taxes (see Luke 20:22-25, Romans 13:7), to make financial investments (see Proverbs 6:6, 19:14, Matthew 25:27, 2 Corinthians 12:14), and to pay for our living expenses (Ecclesiastes 5:18-19, Acts 14:16-17, 1 Timothy 6:17). God uses His system of tithes and offerings to deliver good things to His people. For those who honor Him with their tithe, God increases their income and decreases their expenses (see Malachi 3:10-11). God established the pattern of giving.

We need to learn to receive gifts. When we honor God's system, we maximize our probability of receiving economic resources (see 2 Corinthians 9:6-11). Meditate upon the thought of acquiring wealth through commerce. How do you do this? Deliberately widen your concentration to focus upon selling industrial, intellectual, and investment properties. Consciously think about the numerous ways in which you can create streams of income. Deliberately narrow your concentration to focus upon selling industrial, intellectual, and investment properties. After you have thought about the many different streams of income, narrow your focus to the one you will now pursue. Consider the streams that may likely be most lucrative. Too many people widen their gaze, but they never narrow their focus enough. They major in business administration, but they never focus on what business. Many focus on selling their industrial property, but not enough focus on selling their intellectual and investment properties.

God provides instructions as to how to maximize our economic enjoyments. God does not want us to surrender to economic misfortune. Stop being a victim! It is not the will of God for your economic resources to become depleted. He is not the creator of economic misfortune.

God wants us to transform economic misfortune into a wealth-building experience (see Genesis 41:53-47:28). Joseph used a famine to make Egypt wealthy. In the midst of a seven-year famine, Egypt had plenty. How did Joseph do that? He made Egypt wealthy through the selling of both intellectual and industrial properties. When industrial properties are in low demand, utilize your intellectual properties to improve your economic standing. Providing what is in great demand but in short supply is one basis for building wealth. In this instance, food was in short supply but in great demand. Therefore, people were willing to buy while Joseph had resources to sell.

Some criticize Joseph for becoming wealthy. They reason that he should not have become wealthy at the expense of the poor. Through this experience, however, he saved the world. Therefore we should compliment him.

We should not criticize the wealthy, who have learned the principle of commerce and have successfully engaged therein. Keep ownership of land. Buy land during a famine. In the midst of economic misfortune, sell your intellectual and industrial property to accumulate investment property. Untie your economic progression from political pundits. Place your economic progression solely upon the principles of God

Chapter 12

GOD IS OUR SOURCE

OD OWNS ALL THE ECONOMIC RESOURCES, "FOR the earth is the Lord's, and all it contains" (1 Corinthians 10:26). He possesses the power to give us all we need. Regardless of the view from Wall Street or your street, God is not broke and He is not about to go broke.

Believe the promises of God and see Him as the source of our blessings. Although God may use our employer to compensate us, He is the ultimate source of our reward. "How much more will He clothe you?" (Luke 12:28).

God works through the system of His design. Even to deliver economic resources to His people, God still works through the system of His design. Therefore, we must learn the economic system of God's design. Knowledge is a key factor that determines our economic outcome. Reposition yourself to where the economic resources are available. When the famine came in the land, Abraham left and went down into Egypt (see Genesis 12:10). Although I believe that Abram's going into Egypt was according to God's tolerance, not His preference, nevertheless Abram came out of Egypt very rich. "So Abram went up from Egypt to the Negev, he and his wife and all that belonged to him, and Lot with him. Now Abram was very rich in livestock, in silver and in gold" (Genesis 13:1-2). In the midst of an economic downturn, God's man became rich.

 Avoid all conversation based on fear and worry. Always state the economic solutions, not the economic problems.

You should always prepare for the future. Do you remember Pharaoh's dream? If Joseph's brothers had had knowledge of the upcoming famine, they could have stockpiled food in Canaan and would never have become slaves in Egypt (see Genesis 41:25-47:26). In the midst of an economic downturn, God's man became rich.

You should always avoid all conversation based on fear and worry. Always state the economic solutions, not the economic problems. During this time, increase and intensify your worship and service to God.

What would a farmer do who desires to have a greater harvest? While praying for a climate conducive to a good harvest, he would plant more seed and cultivate the ground better. What should a believer do who desires even greater blessings from God? You cannot reduce your favorable expressions toward God and expect Him to increase His favorable response toward you. During this time, increase and intensify your worship and service to God. Although gas prices are up, do not let the number of your worship attendances go down. God is the source of all your blessings. You cannot reduce your faith reactions toward God and expect Him to increase His grace actions toward you.

> *"Yours, O Lord, is the greatness and the power and the glory and the victory and the majesty, indeed everything that is in the heavens and the earth; Yours is the dominion, O Lord, and You exalt Yourself as head over all. Both riches and honor come from You, and You rule over all, and in Your hand is power and might; and it lies in Your hand to make great and to strengthen everyone"* (1 Chronicles 29:11-12).

As layoffs, foreclosures, and rising prices run rampant, the hearts of many tremble. Obviously, there is reason for the nation to be concerned—but what are believers to do? Believers are to believe the promise of God. He promises to take care of His people. He promised to bless those who would bless Abraham (see Genesis 12:3). In other words, God says, "Do what is right and I will take care of you." We must wholeheartedly believe that truth. Like good stewards, keep using your God-given abilities to manage your God-given resources to accomplish the God-intended results.

How do we reconcile the promise of God with the fact that famine and poverty do exist? God is the source of all our blessings. He possesses the power to give us all we need. Early scriptures clearly document this fact (see 1 Chronicles 29:11-12, 14, 25, 26-28). And the latter scriptures clearly document this fact (see 1 Corinthians 4:7). God works through the system of His design to bring about economic prosperity. Had Joseph's brothers known that a famine was coming, they too would have stockpiled food in Canaan.

We must always be wise to the things of God. We must always make the kingdom of God a priority (see Matthew 6:33). When His Kingdom is a priority within us, God graciously blesses us. First, we must first invest within the kingdom of God before any other expenditures (see Proverbs 3:9-10, 11:24-25, Deuteronomy 14:23). Read my books, *God Knows, Show Me the Money, The Power of the Tongue, Faith, Family, and Finances (Volume One), Success Is a God Idea,* and *My God.* These will fortify your faith and provide you with specific instructions to help you succeed during distressing times.

Second, we must understand that God sustains us because of His promise not because of our performance (Deuteronomy 8:15-18). Even during times of lack, God still distributes relationship and recuperation gifts. Do not become bitter toward those who have or appear to have resources. And remember, tough times do not last, but tough people do.

As layoffs, foreclosures, and rising prices run rampant, the hearts of many tremble. Some leading economic indicators suggest that we are in the midst of and headed for grave economic times. This Web site provides statistical data on the condition of productivity, income, employment, productivity, and other pertinent economic areas: www.whitehouse.gov/fsbr/employment.html.

Chapter 13

THE FAITH FACTOR INCREASES OUR FINANCES

I N MATTHEW CHAPTER 25, THERE ARE THREE END-OF-time parables: the parable of the ten virgins, the parable of the talents, and the parable of sheep and goats. The parable of the talents emphasized accountability. A talent was a piece of money. It weighed approximately 200 pounds. A talent of gold was equivalent to fifteen years' worth of wages. Before going on a journey, a certain lord entrusted his money to his three servants (see verses 14-15). One servant received one talent (200 pounds of gold), another servant received two talents (400 pounds of gold), and yet another servant received five talents (1,000 pounds of gold). Two servants proved to be faithful (see verses 20-23). For them, faith provided a better quality of life. Faithfulness improves our quality of life. To be faithful is to fulfill assigned responsibilities (see Ephesians 6:21-22). Ability + availability + opportunity = assigned responsibility.

 To be fearful is to be faithless. Fear and faithlessness rob us of our productivity.

Our faithfulness affects what we have. Initially, one servant had only five talents (see Matthew 25:15). Subsequently, he had ten talents (see Matthew 25:16, 20, 28). Initially, another servant had only two talents (see verse 15). Subsequently, he had four talents (see verses 17, 22). Initially, one servant had the ability to manage five talents (see verse 15). Subsequently, he developed the ability to manage ten talents (see verses 28-29). Initially, another servant had the ability to manage two talents (see verse 15). Subsequently, he had the ability to manage four (see verse 17).

Our faithfulness affects what we hear. One faithful servant heard, "Well done" (verses 20-21). Another faithful servant heard, "Well done" (verses 22-23). One faithful servant heard, "Good and faithful" (verses 20-21). Another faithful servant heard, "Good and faithful" (verses 22-23).

FEARFUL AND FAITHLESSNESS

In the parable of the talents, one servant received one talent (200 pounds of money). That servant proved to be fearful and faithless (see verse 25). For him, fear provided a lesser quality of life. Fear erodes our quality of life. To be fearful is to be faithless. Fear and faithlessness rob us of our productivity. It causes us to waste our time and energy. The servant who received one talent wasted his time while his lord was away (see verses 14, 19). He also wasted his energy digging in the earth to bury his lord's talent (see verse 18) and to retrieve his lord's talent (see verse 25).

Fear and faithlessness rob us of our presentation. They determine what we visibly and verbally present. Fear limited what the servant visibly presented. On the day of reckoning, he had nothing extra to present (see verse 25). Also, fear limited him to a critical analysis of the character of his lord (see verse 24b) and the conduct of his lord (see verse 24c).

Fear can be defined as "Fantasized Experiences Appearing Real," or FEAR. Fears are self created when we imagine some negative outcome. You can overcome your fears. First, write a list of things you are afraid to do. For example, "I am afraid to drive on I-285." Restate that fear in faith format: "I want to drive and I scare myself by imagining that I will have a wreck on I-285 during rush-hour traffic." Then, scale down the risk: "I will drive on Sunday morning when there is no rush-hour traffic." When you can do that, take another faith step until you can drive on I-285 in rush-hour traffic without fear.

God expects each of us to overcome our fears and work while waiting. Failure to overcome our fears and use our maximum abilities while waiting may result in exclusion from the Kingdom. Always use your maximum abilities. Using your present maximum ability increases your future maximum ability.

KEEP THE FAITH

No doubt, every person has heard about the much discussed condition of our human economy and has decided how he or she will think, feel, and respond. Many facts and factors announce that the economy is in, and may be headed for, even more dire straits. Whereas believers are to operate within the "human" economy, we are not to trust in it. Rather we are to trust in the God of the universe who supersedes our human economy. "Instruct those...not to...fix their hope on the uncertainty of riches, but on God, who richly supplies us with all things to enjoy" (1 Timothy 6:17).

How would God want us to prepare and respond to economic challenges? The study of the story of Joseph provides valuable insight. To prepare for the upcoming famine, God instructed Joseph to take from the people one-fifth (20 percent) of their produce (income) for each of their seven years of plenty (see Genesis 41:34). This percent would serve as a reserve for each of the seven years of famine (see verse 36). Twenty percent for seven years is equivalent to 10 percent for fourteen years. In essence, God recommended doubling the equivalent of their tithe in order to have resources during the time of famine. We, too, should prepare for the time of scarcity by planting more seed during the time of plenty.

What you plant now determines what you harvest later. Within Scripture, does God ever present a person who has nothing to give? Does God know any such category of person? Humanly speaking, you would think that a destitute widow would be unable to give. "But she said,...'I have no bread, only a handful of flour in the bowl and a little oil in the jar; and behold, I am gathering a few sticks that I may go in and prepare for me and my son, that we may eat it and die'" (1 Kings 17:12). Nevertheless, God instructed her to give away a portion of what she had (see verse 13). When she planted a seed from her meager means, God multiplied the seed she planted (see verses 14-16). Because of her willingness to trust God, she and her son went from poverty to prosperity. Jesus commended a widow who gave all that she had. "For they all put in out of their surplus, but she, out of her poverty, put in all she owned, all she had to live on" (Mark 12:44).

Giving is an exercise of faithful trust in God. Therefore the person who offers thanks for the offering should challenge the people to give liberally and remind them of their promised blessings for their faithful giving. May you be blessed as you continue in your generous giving!

God sent twelve men to spy out the promised land of Canaan (see Numbers 13:1-20). Ten spies returned, spoke fearfully, and discouraged the people (see Numbers 13:31-33,

14:1-4, 10). Because of their faithlessness, God repossessed His land (see Numbers 14:11-12).

Caleb, one of the spies, entered a mountainous region of the promised land called Hebron (see Numbers 13:21-22, 14:24). He returned and spoke faithfully to encourage the people (see Numbers 13:30, 14:6-9). Because of Caleb's faithfulness, God promised him the inheritance of the mountainous region of Hebron (see Numbers 14:20-24, 30).

Some forty-five years later, Caleb reminded Joshua of that promise of God (see Joshua 14:6-10). Some forty-five years later, Caleb claimed his promise from God (see verses 11-12). Some forty-five years later, God made good on His promise (see verses 13-14). God intimately interests Himself in your welfare. Therefore, He faithfully keeps His promises.

God had a promised mountain for His people. Hebron had been a worshiping place. There Abraham had built an altar and offered a sacrifice, ratifying God's covenant with him (see Genesis 13:14-18). Hebron had been a weeping place. Abraham buried Sarah there (see Genesis 23:19). Isaac and Ishmael buried Abraham there (see Genesis 25:7-10). Esau and Jacob buried Isaac (see Genesis 35:27-29), and Joseph buried Jacob there (see Genesis 50:13).

God has a promised people for His mountain. Caleb followed God fully (see Numbers 14:24). To follow God fully is to narrow the gap as a hunter narrows the gap between himself and his prey. Because Caleb followed God fully, he inherited this mountain (see Numbers 14:24, 32:11-12, Deuteronomy 1:35-36, Joshua 14:8-9, 14).

> God wants you to trust Him enough to try
> Him. When you try Him, you will become
> convinced of His trustworthiness.

Because Caleb followed God fully, he had a different spirit (see Numbers 14:24). He had a spirit that believed in the statement of God. Because he followed God fully, he had a different speech (see Numbers 13:30, 14:-9). He had a speech that believed in the strength of God (see Joshua 14:11). God's strength was as it was forty-five years earlier.

A faith-filled spirit develops faithful speech. Your speech indicates your spirit. Your speech will determine whether you live in the mountain or die in the wilderness. Have you talked yourself out of the mountain? Your speech will determine whether others live on the mountain or die in the wilderness. Have you talked others out of the mountain?

God wants you to trust Him enough to try Him. When you try Him, you will become convinced of His trustworthiness. When the Israelites discovered they were in a dilemma, they cried out to God. He did not immediately reach down and rescue them. He first provided a set of instructions. He told Moses to stretch out his rod over the sea. Through Moses, God informed the Israelites to go forward (see Exodus 14:5-16). Moses followed God's instructions and stretched out his rod over the sea (see verse 21). The Israelites followed God's instructions and went forward (see verse 22). Because they followed God's instructions, they enjoyed freedom from Pharaoh and the Egyptians (see verses 23-31). Can you imagine what would have happened had they disobeyed God's instructions?

As the Israelites progressed toward the land of Canaan, they needed to capture the city of Jericho. Again, God did not immediately remove the city of Jericho from being an obstacle to them. As before, He gave them a set of instructions. He told them to march once around the walls, once a day for six days. On the seventh day, they were to march around the walls seven times, blow their trumpets, and shout.

Joshua led the Israelites in obeying the instructions of God. They marched once around the walls of Jericho, once a day for six days as God had instructed. On the seventh day, they marched around the walls seven times, blew their trumpets, and shouted as God had instructed (see Joshua 6:1-20). Because they followed God's instructions, they witnessed the walls of Jericho fall down and they went in to claim possession of the land.

Naaman, captain of the army of the king of Aram, was a leper (see 2 Kings 5:1). He sought healing from God through the man of God (see verses 2-9). Through the power of God, the man of God gave him a set of instructions. Elisha sent a messenger informing Naaman to go and wash in the Jordan seven times (see verse 10). Again, did you notice that through a set of instructions, God sought to improve Naaman life?

The paralyzed man to whom Jesus said, "Get up, and pick up your pallet and walk," obeyed (Mark 2:9). Thus, he received healing, which produced for him a more enjoyable future. The man with the withered hand to whom Jesus said,

"Stretch out your hand," obeyed (Mark 3:5). Thus, he also received healing, which produced a more enjoyable future for him. At the moment they both heard Jesus' instructions, no doubt each man thought, "The instructions I follow today will determine the future I will enjoy tomorrow."

Yes, God still seeks to improve the earthly quality of human life. Do not expect God to immediately reach in and rescue you from the dilemmas of life, but do expect God to give you a set of instructions that when followed will bring about a better quality of lifestyle.

Jesus honored and obeyed His heavenly Father perfectly (see Hebrews 4:15). Other than Jesus Christ, no person has or will ever live perfectly, never sinning. There has been and still is room for improvement in the lifestyle of every believer. Therefore, the apostle Paul challenged the believers in Thessalonica to excel even more even though they already walked in his instructions (see 1 Thessalonians 4:1). He knew that following instructions would anoint their life with a spirit of excellence.

Chapter 14

SPIRIT OF EXCELLENCE

THE SPIRIT OF EXCELLENCE BRINGS ABOUT economic resources. With divine authority, the apostle Paul instructed the saints at Thessalonica on how to behave. They followed his instructions (see 1 Thessalonians 4:1-2) because they received them as the word of God (see 1 Thessalonians 2:13). Our children know this principle. When little Robert says to his brother, Richard, "Mommy said for you to wash the dishes," Richard complies only because he receives it as a message from Mommy. However, if he believes that Robert is trying to get him to do his own work, Richard does not bother to wash the dishes. As adults, we know this principle. When we believe the authoritative source has spoken, we respond favorably. When we believe the request is not from an authoritative source, we refuse. Therefore, it is crucial that we receive divinely sanctioned instructions as if they are divinely sanctioned. Otherwise, we bring upon ourselves serious penalty for disobeying God.

> Calm down and follow God's set of instructions.

Following instructions pleases God. God declared that faith pleases Him (see Hebrews 11:6). Therefore, following instructions from Paul was an exercise of faith toward God. Although many in the early church already walked in his instructions, the apostle Paul challenged them to excel even more (see 1 Thessalonians 4:1, 10). He challenged the believers to a lifestyle of excellence. Following instructions anoints our lives with a spirit of excellence. Fair and informed parents learn from God how to reward their children.

God seeks to improve our lives by issuing a set of instructions (see Joshua 1:7-8). Time and time again, God issues instructions through which our obedience brings rewards (see Exodus 14:5-16, Joshua 6:1-5, 2 Kings 5:1-10, Mark 2:1-11, Mark 3:1-5b). Atheists who follow instructions will receive when a believer who rebels receives nothing. For example, if an atheist follows the instructions to open a combination lock, he gets the lock to open. A believer who prays but does not follow the instructions will not get the lock to open. So calm down and follow God's set of instructions. Obedience will improve your economic standing.

The instructions you follow today create the future you will enjoy tomorrow (see Ephesians 1:1-3, Exodus 14:21-25, Joshua 6:12-21, 2 Kings 5:11-14, Mark 2:11-12, Mark 3:5c). Following instructions anoints your life with a spirit of excellence. Following appropriate instructions is an exercise of faith toward God. Therefore, when you reject instructions, you are refusing to exercise faith toward God. God responds to your willingness to follow instructions. Therefore, pleasing God should be the root of your guiding principle. God wants you to seek His set of instructions that will bless your life economically.

WHAT IS THE SPIRIT OF EXCELLENCE?

The spirit of excellence is a degree of distinguished discipline. The patriarch Joseph exercised a degree of distinguished discipline (see Genesis 39:6-12). In a moment we will see through the life of Joseph that there is a direct connection between exercising a degree of distinguished discipline and developing our potential and prosperity.

Exercising distinguished discipline is critical. When Potiphar's wife attempted to seduce Joseph, he exercised moral fortitude and said, "No." Daniel exercised a degree of distinguished discipline (see Daniel 1:8-12). He said, "No" to the king's food and wine. Instead he subsisted on a strict vegetarian diet. Jesus exercised a degree of distinguished discipline. He modeled discipline (see Matthew 4:1-2), and, He taught discipline (see Matthew 6:16-18). We must discipline ourselves in order to prioritize the Kingdom.

Distinguished discipline is worthy of admiration and imitation. As a believer, you must begin to exercise distinguished discipline in your financial dealings. God wants your financial dealings to be admired and imitated. Your distinguished discipline is your talking point for evangelism.

On Sunday evening, September, 24, 1974, in Jackson, Tennessee, six police cruisers cornered me as I was driving. Over their bullhorn they demanded that I exit my car while they crouched with their weapons drawn. Without any explanation they put me under arrest, placed me in a squad car, and started to take me to jail. When we reached the next block, they pulled to the curb, put me out, and said, "Sorry you were at the wrong place at the wrong time."

On Tuesday, January 23, 2007, in Atlanta, Georgia, Willie O. "Pete" Williams, 44, was released from prison after serving twenty-three years of a forty-four year sentence for a crime he did not commit.

What do Mr. William's case and my situation have in common? Someone failed to give due diligence to details. In my situation the police were supposed to be looking for a man with the last name Lake who was driving a green, 1967 Mercury Cougar; my last name is Marshall, and I was driving a yellow, 1969 Mercury, Cougar. The spirit of excellence is a degree of distinguished discipline wherein due diligence is given to detail.

The patriarch Joseph attended to details. He noticed the dejected disposition of Pharaoh's former baker and butler (see Genesis 40:6-7). Because he paid attention to the details of their facial expressions, he received an opportunity to interpret their dreams. His correct interpretation of the dreams of the baker and butler paved the path by which someone recommended him to Pharaoh to interpret his dream (see Genesis 41:1-13). It was through interpreting Pharaoh's dream that Joseph was elevated to second in command in all of Egypt. All these opportunities were linked to the giving of due diligence to details. Due diligence to details paid great dividends in the heart of Africa.

Even though the Babylonian army kidnapped Daniel from among the Hebrews in Jerusalem and transported him to Babylon, Daniel gave due diligence to details. As he recalled king Nebuchadnezzar's dream, Daniel noticed the partial foot of clay of one of the images within the dream. That detail contributed significantly to Daniel's interpretation of the king's dream (see Daniel 2:31-43).

Jesus attended to details. His close attention to details enabled Him to amaze those who heard His questions and answers when He remained behind in the temple (see Luke 2:41-51). Jesus taught others to pay attention to details. He taught them to pay attention to details in laying a foundation for building (see Luke 6:46-49).

God pays attention to details. He pays attention to a sparrow that falls to the ground and to the number of hairs on our head (see Luke 12:6-7).

> The demand for giving due diligence to details separates the mature from the immature,

Moses failed to give due diligence to details. On one occasion, God told him to *strike* the rock (see Exodus 17:5-6). On another occasion, God told him to *speak* to the rock (see Numbers 20:8-12). Because Moses failed to pay attention to the details of difference in the instructions, he forfeited his right to enter the promised land.

Why is it necessary to confirm your online password when establishing a new one? What happens when you attempt to log in to your computer but you have misread a dash (-) for an underscore (_), or a "0" (zero) for an "O"? They are similar but yet very different. The demand for giving due diligence to details separates the mature from the immature, the responsible from the irresponsible, those whom the company will promote from those whom the company will not promote. It even separates those whom God will prosper from those whom God will not prosper.

Within your personal life and your professional life, begin to give due diligence to details. Remember to give due diligence to the details of the unsupervised areas of your life. Do you clean the car and leave the glove compartment cluttered? Do you clean the house and leave the closet cluttered? To significantly change your life and lifestyle, you must change something that you do every day. Therefore, every day exercise the necessary discipline by giving as much attention to details as is necessary to successfully improve your economic standing. Although many are presently suffering economic woes at the hands of others, there is still much that each individual can do to minimize the hurt.

Several years ago, I met Sam Harris (not his real name) who owned and operated a construction company. He shared with me how he came to be in business. A few years earlier, Mr. Peterson (not his real name) had observed Sam's dedication to his former employer. Mr. Peterson observed how Sam paid attention to details and was always willing to go the extra mile. Because of Sam's due diligence, Mr. Peterson set up Sam in his own construction business. His first contract was for more than half a million dollars, and he went on to complete many more project, including one for $8,000,000. How did Sam come to be blessed economically? Through his due diligence, he came to receive financial favor.

Now, where is Nehemiah when we need him? Where is the person who will unveil a specific practice that upholds the principle of due diligence? Will this practice take center stage within the heart of our Sunday morning sermon? If not, why not? If not now, then when?

How many seeds are in an apple? There is a limited number of seeds in each apple. Therefore, we can count the number. How many apples are in a seed? There is an unlimited number of apples in each seed. Therefore, we cannot count the number. What really is a seed? A seed is your future potential. Jesus portrayed the word of God as a seed (see Luke 8:11). Your seed is God's gift to you. Your fruit is your gift to God.

The spirit of excellence is a degree of distinguished discipline wherein due diligence is given to details that develop our full potential. Joseph possessed the potential to reign over his brothers in Egypt even while he was in the pit (see Genesis 37:5-10, 23-24). Joseph possessed the potential to rescue his brother in Egypt even while he was in prison (see Genesis 39:20). Neither time, while he was in the pit nor while in prison, had he developed his full potential.

Joseph noticed the facial expression of the baker and butler (see Genesis 40:6-7). He noted that the king's dream was repeated twice (see Genesis 41:32). Joseph exercised a distinguished disciplined wherein he gave due diligence to details that developed his full potential. Following instructions really does anoint your lifestyle with a spirit of excellence. The spirit of excellence is a degree of distinguished discipline, wherein due diligence is given to details that develop your full potential.

Chapter 15

DEVELOP YOUR POTENTIAL

D EVELOPING YOUR FULL POTENTIAL ENABLES you to be the best you can be. Yes, develop your character—your willingness to do what is right, as God defines right—regardless of the cost. Character causes you to do right simply because it is right to do right. Developing your full potential enables you not only to be the best you can be, but to do the best you can do. Develop your performance. Never render a less-than-your-best performance. The world emphasizes doing and being, wherein doing (performance) is primary, but the kingdom of God emphasizes being and doing; being (character), however, is of primary importance.

Discipline yourself to give due diligence to details that create a climate conducive for seed germination, growth, and production. Sometimes an early frost kills fruit before it ripens. Therefore, you must give due diligence to details until the fruit of your potential fully ripens. God wants you to discipline yourself to give due diligence to the details that create a climate conducive for seed germination, growth, and production. Sometimes, early frost kills fruit before it ripens. Therefore, you must give due diligence to details until the seed that is your potential germinates, grows, and ripens.

Prosperity is the God-caused success in all areas of your life (see Genesis 24:56, Deuteronomy 8:11-18). Regularly we sing that God is so good, but what good has God caused to manifest within your life? The spirit of excellence is a degree of distinguished discipline wherein due diligence is given to details that develop your full potential and promotes prosperity.

Joseph exercised a degree of distinguished discipline wherein he gave due diligence to details that developed his potential and promoted his prosperity. God caused him to succeed in all areas of life (see Genesis 39:1-6). Let's trace Joseph's steps toward prosperity.

 Excellence is not just an event, but rather a process.

Indeed Joseph exercised a distinguished discipline (see Genesis 39:6-12). He gave due diligence to details (see Genesis 40:6-7). While doing so, he developed his full potential. The development of his full potential promoted his prosperity (see Genesis 39:1-3). He came to Egypt as a slave (see Genesis 37:23-28). He was sold into Africa while our ancestors were sold out of Africa. When he arrived, just like our ancestors, he had no (1) citizenship, (2) family, (3) money, (4) rights, (5) status, nor (6) knowledge of Egyptian culture—yet Joseph became second in charge in all Egypt.

Daniel also exercised a degree of distinguished discipline wherein he gave due diligence to details that developed his potential and promoted his prosperity. God caused him to succeed in all areas of life (see Daniel 1:17). Let's trace Daniel's steps toward prosperity. He came into Babylon as a slave (see verse 6). He was sold into Asia while our ancestors were sold out of Africa. When he arrived, just like our ancestors, he had no (1) citizenship, (2) family, (3) money, (4) rights, (5) status, nor (6) knowledge of Babylonian culture—yet because Daniel exercised a degree of distinguished discipline, he rose successfully in Babylon (see Daniel 1:8, 19-20, 2:26-28, 48, 5:13-17, 29, 6:1-4, 28, 10:1-3).

Excellence is not just an event, but rather a process. Because God had anointed his life with the spirit of excellence, Daniel received promotion after promotion in spite of many adversities (see Daniel 2:48, 5:29, 6:1-3, 28). His counterparts envied his prosperity and searched for a way to discredit him. First they sought for negligence in the professional side of his life and then in the personal side of his life (see Daniel 6:4-5).

You must pursue the spirit of excellence in both the professional and personal sides of your life. Pursuing excellence in all of life will drive you to be on time always. Failure to be on time creates a feeling of vulnerability, which may cause you to violate the commandment of God. God legislated that sacrifices be offered by the descendants of Jacob's son, Levi (see Exodus 28:1). Saul was a descendant of Jacob's son, Benjamin (see 1 Samuel 9:1). Because Samuel was late, Saul attempted to do what he should not have done (see 1 Samuel 13:5-14).

Failure to be on time closes the door of opportunity. A closed door of opportunity may cause one to miss the joys of Kingdom living (see Matthew 25:1-10). What is CP time? What is the use of CP time? What are the causes of this habitual lateness? Habitual tardiness stems from a lack of integrity. Habitual tardiness dishonors the essence of the event. It says that the event is not important enough for you to be on time. Habitual tardiness dishonors the participants of the event (those whom you make wait). Those who are habitually late are often "flexing their muscles" just to exercise their power to make others wait.

Habitual tardiness stems from a lack of self-discipline. Those who are undisciplined often will not prepare in advance, and therefore, they find themselves running short on time. Or they may be guilty of not starting out on time, which would give them a larger window of time.

How do we cure habitual lateness? Do not think in terms of just being *on time* but think in terms of being *early.*

Behave not only in terms of just being *on time* but behave in terms of being *early.* Locate the place the day before and determine how long it takes to arrive and build in extra time.

From July 1981 to April 1982, my wife, Priscilla, our three small children, and I drove seventy-five miles to church each way every Sunday morning and Wednesday evening. We traveled from Memphis, Tennessee, to Jonesboro, Arkansas— and were never late. We developed a system. Each week we followed that system.

Tardiness may have already reduced your economic standing. Once, I denied a man the opportunity to earn $400,000 because he was habitually late. He always arrived late and always offered an excuse.

Daniel set his heart against defiling himself with the king's choice of food (see Daniel 1:8-16). Rather he chose a strict vegetarian diet. Daniel's discipline brought about a radiantly convincing appearance. Our appearance is important to God. Why does God concern Himself with our appearance? What strikes the eye? Our appearance makes a first impression (see 1 Samuel 16:1-7). Samuel had no prior knowledge of Eliab. Without any prior knowledge of him, Samuel thought that God's anointing was upon Eliab simply because of his appearance.

What? The Lord looks but at the inward heart, but man looks but at the outward appearance.

Who? When we are trying to persuade God toward man, we must provide what God looks at. God looks at the heart. Therefore, to persuade God we must provide a good heart. When we are trying to persuade man toward God, however, we must provide what man looks at. Since man looks at the outward, we must provide a good outward appearance. We are here to persuade men (see 2 Corinthians 5:11). We are ambassadors and residential representatives on earth, and our mission is to convince the unbelieving world of God (see 2 Corinthians 5:20, 1 Corinthians 14:24-25).

Your appearance makes a firm impression (see Genesis 38:1-26). Your appearance may cause someone to think you are who you are not (see Genesis 38:15, 20-22). Or your appearance may cause someone to treat you like you are not (see verses 16, 26).

God expects you to present a convincing appearance. God did not give you the ability to read others' hearts, except through their outward appearance. God did not give you the ability to reveal your own heart, except through outward appearance. God decided that you would use outward appearance to convince others. Since you are on earth to impress and persuade man, your appearance can never be less than excellent for God's sake. God expects you to present your most convincing appearance while praising Him for the specific prosperity that He has granted due to your spirit of excellence.

Growing up on the farm taught me life-long lessons.

How does this affect your finances? The financial instructions you follow today will create the economic future you will enjoy tomorrow. Most of your present enjoyments are inherently connected to your past actions. There is not only a correlation between your past actions and your present enjoyments, but there is also a cause-and-effect relationship.

Following instructions really does anoint your life with a spirit of excellence. Following appropriate instructions is an exercise of faith toward God. Therefore, those who reject instructions are refusing to exercise faith toward God. When the writer of the book of Hebrews said, "And without faith it is impossible to please Him" (Hebrews 11:6), he also told us that without following instructions it is impossible to please Him.

Did I tell you that I am a farmer by birth, concrete finisher and brick layer by trade, and that I just happen to be serving God in the ministry? If not, I have now. Growing up on the farm taught me life-long lessons. Every farmer knows that honoring God's design is the only way to have an increased harvest. First, you must plant more seed if you want a greater harvest. Second, you must trust God to multiply your seed sown. Third, you must manage your harvest so as to retain some of it until after your next crop has begun to ripen. Now you have it, from right in front of the horse's eyes.

Earlier in this book I wrote there was "fire shut up in my bones" that would not allow me to hold my peace—and compelled me to pen these words. Like the days of Nehemiah, the protective walls around us have been breached, and God is calling us to rebuild them "so that we will no longer be a reproach" (Nehemiah 2:17b).

Thank you for allowing me to speak passionately and truthfully about how I believe the church has responded to sin and to saints who sin—and how we must respond if we are to repair the damage done and fix the mess we are in.

We need a Nehemiah in our day. Yes, our generation longs for someone like Nehemiah who can see the mess that we are in, leaving saints to fend for themselves. Not only do we need a Nehemiah who can see the mess we are in, but we need a Nehemiah who will speak the message that will lead us out of the mess we are in. Yes, we need a Nehemiah who will look the saints who sin non-judgmentally in the eye, and say with correction, "You should not have done it. But now that you have done it, I am going to walk with you all the way out of this sin. Now let's get moving because time is a-wasting." Then when the saint has walked out of the sin, remind him or her that their sin sentence has been commuted without probation.

It is my sincere prayer that within this book you have discovered the building blocks that will not only move your heart as to the principles, but more importantly move you to action in practicing the principles. Although the assignment of "getting out of the mess we have made" of our faith, family, and finances may seem to be a daunting one, this broken wall can be rebuilt. It can be done when we put to practice the principles that we teach. It can be done when we divide the tasks of repairing the body of Christ among the body of Christ (see Nehemiah 3). It can be done when we seek to help rather than hinder.

I have spoken the truth because I, like Jeremiah, am weary of this fire shut up in my bones, and indeed I cannot hold it in. Not only for the sake of quenching this fire but rather with a heart filled with faith in God and love for His people, I am determined to bring healing to the body of Christ and restoration of our faith, family, and finances.

Other books by John Marshall

Good and Angry
A Personal Guide to Anger Management

God Knows!
There Is No Need to Worry

God, Listen!
Prayers That God Always Answers
(includes addiction-recovery guide)

Final Answer
You Asked, God Answered

My God !
Who He Is Will Change Your Life

The Power of the Tongue
What You Say Is What You Get

Success Is a God Idea

Show Me the Money
7 Exercises That Build Economic Strength

Faith, Family & Finances—Volume One
Essential Truths That Lead to Passionate Happiness

Contact Information

John Marshall
P.O. Box 2136
Stone Mountain GA 30086
(404) 297-9050
jdm@graceview.us

CPSIA information can be obtained
at www.ICGtesting.com
Printed in the USA
LVOW12s0429240516

489518LV00001B/4/P